THE RAG

PROGRAMMING

COOK BOOK

RECIPES FOR

EXPERTS

USING PYTHON

AND LANGCHAIN

WILLIAM K ROBERT

The Rag Programming Cook Book: Recipes for Experts Using Python and Langchain

Table of Contents

10.3 The Master Chef's Touch: Final Thoughts on the Power of Rag Programming Expertise

Chapter 1:

Introduction to the Rag Programming Feast

This chapter lays the groundwork for your journey into the exciting world of Rag programming. We'll whet your appetite with an overview of what Rag programming is and the core principles that make it a powerful tool. Here's a breakdown of the three subsections:

1.1 What's on the Menu? Demystifying Rag Programming

- This section will introduce the concept of Rag programming, explaining its core functionalities and how it streamlines data science workflows.
- We'll break down the acronym "RAG" and delve into the key components involved in this approach.

1.2 Essential Ingredients: Core Concepts and Principles

- Here, we'll explore the fundamental building blocks of Rag programming.
- This includes concepts like retrieval-augmented generation, knowledge base integration, and the role of Langchain in the process.

1.3 A Taste of Success: Benefits and Applications of Rag Programming

- This section will highlight the advantages of using Rag programming compared to traditional methods.
- We'll discuss real-world applications of Rag programming across various domains, showcasing its versatility and impact.

By the end of this chapter, you'll have a clear understanding of Rag programming's foundation and the potential it holds for your data science endeavors.

1.1 What's on the Menu? Demystifying Rag Programming

Welcome to the world of Rag programming, where you'll be a master chef crafting powerful data science solutions! This section serves as your appetizer, introducing the core concept of Rag programming and its role in streamlining your data science workflow.

The Art of Rag Programming:

Imagine a data scientist who juggles multiple tasks: gathering information, preparing data, and building models. Rag programming acts as your sous chef, automating and optimizing these processes. It's a technique that combines two key elements:

Retrieval: Think of this as gathering the freshest ingredients (data) from various sources. Rag programming retrieves relevant information for your specific task, ensuring your models have the best data at hand.

Augmented Generation: This is like transforming those ingredients into a delicious dish (model). Rag programming utilizes the retrieved data to enhance the creation (generation) of powerful machine learning models.

By combining these elements, Rag programming helps you build more accurate and efficient models, saving you time and effort in the kitchen (data science environment).

Beyond the Basics:

The acronym "RAG" stands for **Retrieval-Augmented Generation**. This emphasizes the core functionality of retrieving data and leveraging it to generate better models.

As we delve deeper into the chapter, we'll explore the specific components involved in Rag programming, including the role of Langchain, a powerful library that streamlines the retrieval and integration of external knowledge.

Stay tuned, the next sections will unveil the essential ingredients (core concepts) and the delectable results (benefits and applications) of Rag programming!

1.2 Essential Ingredients: Core Concepts and Principles

In this section, we'll delve into the heart of Rag programming, exploring the fundamental concepts and principles that make it tick. Imagine these as the key spices and techniques that elevate your data science dish (model) to a whole new level.

Here are some of the essential ingredients we'll explore:

1. Retrieval-Augmented Generation (RAG):

We'll revisit the core concept of RAG, delving deeper into the specific mechanisms of how data retrieval is augmented to generate superior models.

This includes exploring how Rag programming identifies relevant information from external sources and integrates it with your existing data.

2. Knowledge Base Integration:

Rag programming leverages the power of knowledge bases. These are vast repositories of structured information that can provide valuable context and background knowledge for your models.

We'll discuss how Rag programming seamlessly integrates information from knowledge bases, enriching your models with additional insights.

3. Langchain and Distributed Processing:

Langchain plays a crucial role in Rag programming. It's a powerful library that simplifies the process of retrieving and integrating data from various sources.

This section will explore how Langchain facilitates distributed processing, allowing you to handle large datasets efficiently.

4. Model Explainability and Interpretability:

While Rag programming excels at generating powerful models, ensuring their interpretability is crucial.

We'll discuss how Rag programming techniques can help you understand the rationale behind your models' predictions, fostering trust and reliability.

5. Continuous Learning and Adaptation:

The world of data is constantly evolving. Here, we'll explore how Rag programming can be used to create models that continuously learn and adapt to new information.

This ensures your models remain relevant and effective in a dynamic environment.

By understanding these core ingredients, you'll gain a deeper appreciation for the power and potential of Rag programming in your data science endeavors. The next section will showcase the delicious results you can achieve with this approach.

1.3 A Taste of Success: Benefits and Applications of Rag Programming

Now that you've explored the essential ingredients of Rag programming, it's time to savor the delectable results! This section will highlight the key benefits of using Rag programming and showcase its diverse applications across various domains.

_Benefits of Rag Programming:

Enhanced Model Performance: Rag programming empowers you to build more accurate and efficient models by leveraging relevant information from external sources. This can lead to significant improvements in areas like prediction accuracy and generalization.

Streamlined Workflow: Rag programming automates data retrieval and integration tasks, freeing you from manual processes and allowing you to focus on higher-level data science activities.

Improved Model Explainability: By understanding the information retrieved by Rag programming, you can gain insights into the decision-making process of your models, fostering trust and interpretability.

Continuous Learning: Rag programming enables you to create models that can continuously learn and adapt to new data as it becomes available. This ensures your models remain relevant and effective in dynamic environments.

Scalability: Langchain, a key component of Rag programming, facilitates distributed processing, allowing you to handle large datasets efficiently.

_Applications of Rag Programming:

Natural Language Processing (NLP): Rag programming can be used to enhance tasks like sentiment analysis, text summarization, and machine translation by incorporating knowledge from external sources like knowledge bases and text corpora.

Computer Vision: In computer vision applications, Rag programming can be used to improve object recognition and image classification by leveraging external knowledge about objects and their properties.

Recommendation Systems: Rag programming can personalize user experiences in recommendation systems by incorporating user preferences and contextual information from external sources.

Healthcare and Bioinformatics: Rag programming can analyze large datasets of medical records and scientific research, leading to advancements in drug discovery, disease diagnosis, and personalized medicine.

Financial Modeling: Rag programming can be used to build more accurate and robust financial models by incorporating real-time market data and financial news.

As you can see, Rag programming offers a versatile toolkit that can be applied across a wide range of fields. With its ability to enhance model performance, streamline workflows, and promote continuous learning, Rag programming is a powerful addition to any data scientist's arsenal.

Chapter 2:

Prepping Your Kitchen: Setting Up Your Rag Programming Environment

Before you start whipping up delicious data science dishes with Rag programming, you need a well-equipped kitchen (environment). This chapter equips you with the essential tools and ingredients (software) to get started.

Here's a breakdown of the three key sections:

2.1 Installing the Essentials: Configuring Python for Rag Programming

- This section acts as your recipe guide, outlining the steps involved in installing and configuring Python, the foundation of your Rag programming environment.
- We'll cover the installation process for various operating systems, ensuring a smooth setup.
- Additionally, we'll explore essential Python libraries commonly used in the Rag programming workflow.

2.2 Picking the Perfect Tools: Choosing and Integrating Langchain Libraries

- Langchain is your sous chef in the Rag programming kitchen. Here, we'll delve into the world of Langchain libraries, helping you choose the right tools for your specific needs.
- We'll explore popular Langchain libraries like Retriever, Transformer, and Processor, explaining their functionalities and how they integrate seamlessly with your Python environment.

2.3 Mastering the Workflow: Essential Tools and Processes for Rag Programming

- This section is your cheat sheet for mastering the Rag programming workflow.
- We'll explore essential tools beyond Python and Langchain that are commonly used in Rag programming projects.
- Additionally, we'll establish a clear workflow, guiding you through the steps of data preparation, model building, and evaluation – all with a Rag programming twist.

By the end of this chapter, you'll have a fully equipped Rag programming environment ready to tackle any data science challenge.

2.1 Installing the Essentials: Configuring Python for Rag Programming

Just like any good chef needs a well-stocked pantry, your Rag programming journey begins with setting up your Python environment. This section acts as your recipe guide, walking you through the installation and configuration of Python, the foundation of your Rag programming kitchen.

Ingredients (Software):

Python: This is the core ingredient, the versatile language that powers Rag programming.

Package Manager: We'll use a package manager like pip (Python Package Installer) to install additional libraries needed for Rag programming.

_The Recipe (Installation Process):

Download Python: Head over to the official Python website (https://www.python.org/downloads/) and download the latest stable version of Python that's compatible with your operating system (Windows, macOS, or Linux).

Install Python: Follow the on-screen instructions during the installation process. It's generally recommended to keep the "Add Python to PATH" option checked for easier access from the command line.

Verify Installation: Once installed, open a command prompt (Windows) or terminal (macOS/Linux) and type `python --version` or `python3 --version` (depending on your installation). If successful, you'll see the installed Python version displayed.

Essential Spices (Libraries):

In addition to Python, we'll need a few essential libraries to enhance our Rag programming capabilities. We'll install them using the `pip` package manager:

NumPy: Provides powerful numerical computing functionalities. Install with `pip install numpy`.

Pandas: Enables efficient data manipulation and analysis. Install with `pip install pandas`.

Matplotlib/Seaborn: Used for creating data visualizations. Install with `pip install matplotlib` or `pip install seaborn`. (Choose one for visualization)

Tip: Keep your Python environment up-to-date with the latest libraries using `pip install --upgrade <library_name>`.

By following these steps, you'll have a well-seasoned Python environment ready to explore the exciting world of Rag programming. The next section will introduce you to Langchain, your sous chef in this culinary data science adventure.

2.2 Picking the Perfect Tools: Choosing and Integrating Langchain Libraries

Langchain is your secret weapon in the Rag programming kitchen. It's a powerful library suite that streamlines the retrieval and integration of external knowledge for your data science projects. Imagine Langchain as your expert sous chef, efficiently gathering the right ingredients (data) to enhance your dishes (models).

Here, we'll delve into the world of Langchain libraries, helping you choose the perfect tools for your specific culinary data science needs.

The Langchain Pantry:

Langchain offers a variety of specialized libraries, each with its own role in the Rag programming workflow. Let's explore some of the most commonly used ones:

Retriever: This library acts like your highly skilled prep cook, efficiently searching and retrieving relevant information from various external sources. It can access knowledge bases, public datasets, and even the web to gather the data your models need.

Transformer: Think of this as your master chef's special tool. The Transformer library takes the retrieved information and processes it, transforming it into a format that seamlessly integrates with your machine learning models.

Processor: This library acts as your meticulous cleaner and organizer. It ensures the retrieved and transformed data is properly formatted and prepared for use in your models. The Processor cleans, preprocesses, and tokenizes the data, making it ready for the machine learning algorithms.

Picking the Right Tools:

The specific Langchain libraries you'll use depend on your project's requirements. Here's a quick guide to choosing the right tools:

For Text-Based Tasks: If you're working with text data and want to leverage knowledge bases or textual information retrieval, the Retriever and Transformer libraries will be your go-to choices.

For Structured Data Integration: If your project involves integrating data from databases or APIs, the Retriever and Processor libraries will be most useful.

Seamless Integration:

Langchain integrates smoothly with your Python environment. We'll explore the installation process for Langchain and demonstrate how to use these libraries in conjunction with your Python code. This will equip you to leverage the power of external knowledge retrieval and data integration for your Rag programming projects.

The next section will explore the essential workflow for Rag programming, guiding you through the steps of data preparation, model building, and evaluation – all with a Rag programming twist.

2.3 Mastering the Workflow: Essential Tools and Processes for Rag Programming

Now that your kitchen is stocked with Python and Langchain (your sous chef!), it's time to master the essential workflow for Rag programming. This section unveils the key steps involved in crafting delicious data science dishes (models) using the Rag programming approach.

Here's a breakdown of the essential processes involved:

1. Data Preparation with a Rag Programming Twist:

Data Acquisition: This initial step remains crucial. You'll gather your core dataset relevant to your project's objective.

Data Cleaning and Preprocessing: As usual, data cleaning and preprocessing techniques like handling missing values and outliers are essential.

Leveraging Langchain for External Knowledge Integration: Here's where Rag programming shines! Use Langchain's Retriever library to identify and retrieve relevant information from external sources like knowledge bases or APIs. This could involve fetching related articles, entity descriptions, or complementary datasets that enrich your core data.

Data Augmentation with Retrieved Information: Incorporate the retrieved information from Langchain into your core dataset. This can involve feature engineering techniques or simply merging the data in a meaningful way.

2. Model Building with Rag Programming Enhancement:

Choose Your Machine Learning Model: Select the machine learning model best suited for your task (e.g., classification, regression). Popular choices include neural networks, support vector machines, or random forests.

Integrate Retrieved Knowledge: Here, Rag programming's magic unfolds. Leverage the knowledge retrieved by Langchain to enhance your model. This could involve incorporating the retrieved information as additional features, using it to pre-train your model, or even guiding the model architecture selection.

3. Evaluation and Refinement:

Evaluate Model Performance: Test and evaluate your model's performance using appropriate metrics relevant to your task. Analyze factors like accuracy, precision, recall, or F1-score.

Refine and Iterate: Based on the evaluation results, refine your model by adjusting hyperparameters, exploring different Rag programming techniques for knowledge integration, or potentially even trying a different machine learning model altogether.

Beyond the Basics:

Version Control: Consider using version control systems like Git to track changes in your code and data throughout the Rag programming workflow. This allows for easier collaboration and facilitates revisiting previous versions if needed.

Experimentation: Don't be afraid to experiment with different Langchain libraries, retrieval strategies, and knowledge integration techniques. The best approach often depends on the specific problem you're trying to solve.

By mastering these essential workflow steps and incorporating the power of Langchain for external knowledge retrieval, you'll be well on your way to creating powerful and effective models using Rag programming. Let's explore the exciting world of Rag programming applications in the next chapter!

Chapter 3:

Data Wrangling Delights: Mastering Data with Rag Programming

Data wrangling is often the groundwork for successful data science projects. In Rag programming, however, it becomes an opportunity to add flavor and richness to your machine learning models. This chapter delves into how Rag programming elevates data wrangling from a chore to a culinary art form, transforming raw data into the perfect ingredients for your models.

Here's a breakdown of the three key sections we'll explore:

3.1 Cleaning Up the Mess: Data Cleaning and Preprocessing Techniques

- We'll revisit the fundamentals of data cleaning and preprocessing, essential steps for ensuring the quality of your core data.
- Techniques like handling missing values, identifying and correcting outliers, and dealing with inconsistencies will be covered.

3.2 Building Efficient Pipelines: Streamlining Data Transformation

- This section focuses on efficiency. We'll explore how to build streamlined data transformation pipelines using Python libraries like Pandas.
- You'll learn how to automate repetitive data cleaning tasks and create reusable functions for common transformations.

3.3 Scaling Up Your Feast: Leveraging Langchain for Scalable Data Handling

- As your datasets grow larger and more complex, Rag programming shines. Here, we'll introduce Langchain's role in handling big data.
- We'll explore how Langchain can be used to parallelize data processing tasks across multiple machines, allowing you to efficiently wrangle even the most massive datasets.

Mastering the Art of Data Wrangling:

Data wrangling is a crucial yet often tedious step in data science. Rag programming, however, injects excitement into the process by allowing you to incorporate valuable external knowledge during data preparation. Imagine using information from external sources to enrich your data and enhance your models' understanding of the problem.

Adding Spice to Your Data:

Here are some ways Rag programming can be used to elevate your data wrangling skills:

Entity Linking: Imagine being able to automatically identify and link entities (like people, places, or organizations) within your data to relevant entries in a knowledge base. Langchain's Retriever library can help you achieve this, enriching your data with additional context and meaning.

Knowledge Base Augmentation: Let's say you're working with customer reviews. Rag programming allows you to leverage knowledge bases containing product information or sentiment lexicons. This can be used to create new features or improve the quality of existing ones in your dataset.

Text Augmentation: For tasks involving text data, Rag programming can be used to enrich your data by retrieving relevant text snippets or documents from external sources. This can be particularly useful for tasks like sentiment analysis or text summarization.

By incorporating these techniques, you'll transform data wrangling from a chore into a strategic step for crafting powerful Rag programming models. The next section will delve into the art of feature engineering, where Rag programming truly adds its magic touch.

3.1 Cleaning Up the Mess: Data Cleaning and Preprocessing Techniques (with code examples)

Just like any chef meticulously cleans and prepares ingredients before cooking, data cleaning and preprocessing are essential steps in Rag programming. This section equips you with the tools to handle the inevitable messiness of real-world data, ensuring your models have the best foundation for success.

The Cleaning Crew:

Data cleaning involves identifying and correcting errors, inconsistencies, and missing values within your dataset. Here are some common techniques you'll encounter, along with code examples using the popular Pandas library in Python:

1. Missing Value Imputation:

Mean/Median Imputation: Replace missing values with the average (mean) or median value of the column.

Python

```
import pandas as pd
```

```
# Load sample data with missing values
data = pd.read_csv("sample_data.csv")

# Impute missing values in the 'price' column
with the mean
data["price"].fillna(data["price"].mean(),
inplace=True)

# Impute missing values in the 'age' column with
the median
data["age"].fillna(data["age"].median(),
inplace=True)
```

Langchain for Missing Value Imputation (Example): While not directly supported in Pandas, Langchain can be used to retrieve relevant information from external sources to potentially fill in missing values more intelligently. This could involve using knowledge bases or similar resources to find typical values for specific entities within your data.

2. Outlier Detection and Treatment:

Identifying Outliers: Use statistical methods like Interquartile Range (IQR) to identify data points that fall outside a specific range.

Python

```
# Calculate quartiles for the 'income' column
Q1 = data["income"].quantile(0.25)
Q3 = data["income"].quantile(0.75)
```

```
# Identify outliers based on IQR
IQR = Q3 - Q1
lower_bound = Q1 - 1.5 * IQR
upper_bound = Q3 + 1.5 * IQR
outliers = data[(data["income"] < lower_bound) |
(data["income"] > upper_bound)]

# Explore or handle outliers (e.g., remove, cap,
winsorize)
```

3. Data Type Conversion:

Convert data types: Use Pandas functions like `astype` to convert data types (e.g., string to numeric).

Python

```
# Convert the 'purchase_date' column to datetime
format
data["purchase_date"]                              =
pd.to_datetime(data["purchase_date"])

# Convert the 'category' column from string to
categorical type
data["category"]                                   =
data["category"].astype("category")
```

4. Normalization and Standardization:

Normalization: Scale data to a specific range (e.g., 0 to 1).

Python

```python
from sklearn.preprocessing import MinMaxScaler

# Normalize the 'age' column between 0 and 1
scaler = MinMaxScaler(feature_range=(0, 1))
data["age_normalized"]                          =
scaler.fit_transform(data[["age"]])
```

Standardization: Convert data to have a mean of 0 and standard deviation of 1.

Python

```python
from sklearn.preprocessing import StandardScaler

# Standardize the 'income' column
scaler = StandardScaler()
data["income_standardized"]                     =
scaler.fit_transform(data[["income"]])
```

The Power of Consistency:

Data inconsistencies can lead to errors in your models. Here's how to address them:

Handling Formatting Issues: Use string manipulation techniques (e.g., regular expressions) to address inconsistencies in formats.

Python

```python
# Remove leading/trailing spaces from the 'name'
column
data["name"] = data["name"].str.strip()
```

```
# Convert all characters in the 'city' column to
lowercase
data["city"] = data["city"].str.lower()
```

Identifying and Correcting Errors: Use validation techniques and data quality checks to identify and correct errors.

Python

```
# Check for duplicate entries in the data
duplicates = data.duplicated()

# Explore and handle duplicate entries (e.g.,
remove or deduplicate)
```

Rag Programming's Twist:

While these techniques are fundamental, Rag programming offers an exciting twist. Leverage Langchain to enrich the data cleaning process:

Identifying Inconsistencies with Knowledge Bases: Use Langchain's Retriever library to query knowledge bases and identify potential inconsistencies in your data based on external information.

Python

```
#  (Placeholder  code)  Simulate  retrieving
inconsistency information from a knowledge base
inconsistencies = langchain.retriever
```

3.2 Building Efficient Pipelines: Streamlining Data Transformation

Data wrangling in Rag programming can involve multiple cleaning, transformation, and manipulation steps. This section dives into the art of building efficient pipelines to streamline these processes. Imagine having a well-oiled machine handling your data preparation, saving you time and effort in the kitchen (data science environment).

The Assembly Line:

Data transformation pipelines act like an assembly line for your data, automating repetitive tasks and ensuring consistency throughout the Rag programming workflow. Here's why they're essential:

Improved Efficiency: By creating reusable functions and chaining data processing steps, you save time and avoid errors caused by repetitive manual coding.

Enhanced Maintainability: Well-structured pipelines are easier to maintain and update as your data or processing needs evolve.

Reproducibility: Pipelines ensure your data preparation process is replicable, fostering trust and collaboration in your projects.

Building Your Pipeline with Pandas:

Pandas is a powerful Python library that excels at data manipulation. Here's a breakdown of the key steps involved in building a data transformation pipeline with Pandas:

Define Functions for Each Transformation Step: Break down your data cleaning and preprocessing tasks into smaller, reusable functions. Each function should perform a specific transformation, like handling missing values or encoding categorical variables.

Python

```python
import pandas as pd

def handle_missing_values(data):
    # Fill missing values using techniques like mean/median imputation
    # ... (implementation details)
    return data

def encode_categorical_variables(data):
    # Encode categorical variables using techniques like one-hot encoding
    # ... (implementation details)
    return data
```

Chain the Functions Together: Use Pandas function chaining to create a sequence of transformations applied to your data.

Python

```python
# Sample data
data = pd.DataFrame({"age": [25, None, 30],
"city": ["New York", "Los Angeles", None]})

# Apply the transformation functions in sequence
clean_data = (
    data
```

```
        .pipe(handle_missing_values)    # Fill missing
values
        .pipe(encode_categorical_variables)    # Encode
categorical variables
)

print(clean_data)
```

Beyond the Basics:

Error Handling: Incorporate error handling mechanisms into your pipelines to gracefully handle unexpected issues during data processing.

Parallelization: For very large datasets, explore libraries like Dask that enable parallel processing of data transformation steps across multiple cores or machines.

Rag Programming Integration:

Rag programming seamlessly integrates with data transformation pipelines. Here's how:

Langchain Integration: Within your pipeline functions, leverage Langchain's libraries to retrieve information from external sources and integrate it into your data transformations.

Python

```
#   (Placeholder   code)   Simulate   retrieving
information from a knowledge base using Langchain
def enrich_data_with_knowledge_base(data):
```

```
    # Retrieve relevant information from a
knowledge base using Langchain's Retriever
library
  # ... (implementation details)
  # Update data with retrieved information
  # ... (implementation details)
  return data

# Integrate the enrichment function into the
pipeline
clean_data = (
    data
    .pipe(handle_missing_values)
    .pipe(encode_categorical_variables)
      .pipe(enrich_data_with_knowledge_base)    #
Leverage Langchain for data enrichment
)
```

By following these steps and incorporating Rag programming's capabilities, you can build efficient and scalable data transformation pipelines that empower you to prepare your data for building powerful models. The next section will explore how Langchain tackles the challenge of handling big data in Rag programming.

3.3 Scaling Up Your Feast: Leveraging Langchain for Scalable Data Handling

As your data grows in volume and complexity, wrangling it can become a daunting task. This section explores how Rag programming's secret weapon, Langchain, empowers you to handle big data efficiently. Imagine being able to prepare a massive feast (large dataset) for your machine learning models without breaking a sweat.

The Big Data Challenge:

Traditional data wrangling techniques can become slow and resource-intensive when dealing with big data. Here are some of the challenges you might encounter:

Processing Time: Traditional methods might take an unreasonable amount of time to process massive datasets, hindering your workflow.

Memory Constraints: Large datasets can easily exceed the memory capacity of a single machine, causing processing errors.

Scalability Limitations: As your data volume increases, traditional methods might not scale effectively, hindering your ability to handle even larger datasets in the future.

Langchain to the Rescue:

Langchain offers several features that make it well-suited for handling big data in Rag programming:

Parallelization: Langchain can distribute data processing tasks across multiple cores or machines, significantly reducing processing time for large datasets. This allows you to leverage the combined processing power of your computing infrastructure.

Lazy Evaluation: Langchain utilizes lazy evaluation, meaning it retrieves and processes data only when necessary. This helps to optimize memory usage and avoid overloading your system.

Modular Design: Langchain's modular architecture allows you to break down complex data processing workflows into smaller, manageable steps. This improves efficiency and simplifies handling big data.

Scaling Your Rag Programming Workflow:

Here's how to leverage Langchain for scalable data handling in Rag programming:

Identify Bottlenecks: Analyze your data wrangling pipeline and identify steps that are particularly time-consuming or memory-intensive for large datasets.

Leverage Langchain's Parallelization: For identified bottlenecks, explore how Langchain's parallelization capabilities can be applied. This could involve distributing data retrieval tasks from external sources or parallelizing data cleaning steps across multiple cores.

Optimize with Lazy Evaluation: Restructure your pipeline functions to take advantage of Langchain's lazy evaluation. This ensures that data is retrieved and processed only when it's truly needed.

Beyond the Basics:

Cloud Integration: Consider using cloud platforms that offer scalable computing resources. Langchain can integrate seamlessly with cloud environments, allowing you to leverage on-demand scalability for handling massive datasets.

Big Data Frameworks: For truly massive datasets, explore big data frameworks like Apache Spark that Langchain can interact with. This enables distributed processing across clusters of machines for ultra-scalable data wrangling.

By understanding Langchain's strengths and incorporating these strategies, you can ensure your Rag programming workflow scales effectively to handle even the most challenging big data problems. In the next chapter, we'll delve into the exciting world of feature engineering, where Rag programming truly shines.

Chapter 4:

Feature Engineering Entrees: Crafting Powerful Features from Data

In the culinary world, the quality of ingredients is essential, but a skilled chef knows the importance of transforming them into delicious dishes. Similarly, in data science, feature engineering plays a crucial role in transforming raw data into features that empower your models to learn effectively. This chapter explores how Rag programming elevates feature engineering to an art form, allowing you to craft the perfect "entrees" (features) for your machine learning models.

Here's a glimpse of the exciting topics we'll explore:

4.1 The Art of Feature Engineering:

- We'll revisit the fundamentals of feature engineering, including techniques for creating new features from existing ones, dimensionality reduction, and feature selection.

4.2 Rag Programming's Special Spices:

- This section unveils the unique capabilities of Rag programming in feature engineering. We'll explore how to leverage external knowledge from knowledge bases and other sources to create powerful features.

4.3 Crafting Features with Langchain:

- We'll delve into practical examples of how Langchain's libraries can be used to retrieve information and integrate it into the feature engineering process.

4.4 Beyond the Recipe: Experimentation and Optimization

- Feature engineering is an iterative process. This section highlights the importance of experimentation and optimization to identify the most effective feature sets for your models.

The Art of Feature Transformation:

Feature engineering involves transforming your raw data into features that are informative and relevant for your machine learning task. Here's a breakdown of some key techniques:

Feature Creation: Derive new features from existing ones. This could involve calculations, transformations, or combining multiple features.

Dimensionality Reduction: If you have a large number of features, dimensionality reduction techniques like Principal Component Analysis (PCA) can help reduce redundancy and improve model performance.

Feature Selection: Not all features are equally important. Feature selection techniques help identify the most relevant features that contribute the most to your model's learning process.

Rag Programming's Special Spices:

While these core techniques are essential, Rag programming adds a unique flavor to feature engineering:

Knowledge Base Integration: Imagine using information from knowledge bases to enrich your features. You could leverage entity linking to connect entities within your data to relevant entries in a knowledge base, extracting additional attributes and relationships.

External Data Augmentation: For specific tasks, Rag programming allows you to retrieve relevant data from external sources (e.g., APIs, public datasets) and incorporate it into your feature creation process. This can be particularly useful for tasks like sentiment analysis or topic modeling.

Text Feature Engineering with External Knowledge: For text-based data, Rag programming allows you to leverage external knowledge sources like sentiment lexicons or topic models to create informative text features.

These capabilities empower you to craft features that are not only informative about the data itself but also incorporate valuable contextual knowledge from the external world.

Crafting Features with Langchain:

Langchain plays a vital role in Rag programming's feature engineering:

Retrieving Information for Feature Creation: Use Langchain's Retriever library to retrieve relevant information from external sources. This information can then be used to create new features or enhance existing ones.

Entity Linking with Langchain: Leverage Langchain to identify and link entities within your data to knowledge bases. The retrieved information about these entities can be used to create informative features.

Text Augmentation with Langchain: For text data, use Langchain to retrieve relevant text snippets or documents from external sources. This can be used to enrich your text features and improve the performance of tasks like sentiment analysis or text summarization.

By incorporating these techniques, you can leverage the power of Langchain to create a rich set of features that unlock the full potential of your machine learning models.

The Importance of Experimentation:

Feature engineering is an iterative process. There's no single "best" set of features for every task. Here's how to optimize your feature engineering approach:

Experiment with Different Techniques: Try various feature creation, dimensionality reduction, and feature selection techniques to identify the most effective combination for your specific problem.

Evaluate Feature Importance: Use techniques like feature importance analysis to understand which features contribute most to your model's performance. This can guide you in refining your feature set.

Domain Knowledge is Key: Leverage your understanding of the problem domain to identify potentially relevant features or external knowledge sources that Rag programming can exploit.

By continuously experimenting and refining your feature engineering approach, you'll ensure that your models have the best possible foundation for success. The next chapter will showcase the power of Rag programming in action, exploring various applications where it can be used to create state-of-the-art machine learning models.

4.1 The Art of Feature Engineering:

Feature engineering is a crucial step in the machine learning workflow that involves transforming raw data into features that are informative and relevant for a specific machine learning task. Just like a skilled chef meticulously prepares ingredients to enhance a dish, feature engineering sets the stage for your machine learning models to learn effectively.

Here, we'll delve into the essential concepts and techniques involved in feature engineering:

_Feature Creation: This involves deriving new features from existing ones in your data. There are various creative ways to achieve this, including:

Mathematical transformations: Apply mathematical functions (e.g., logarithm, square root) to existing features to create new ones.

Feature combinations: Combine existing features to create new informative features. For example, you might create a feature representing the ratio between two existing features.

Feature interaction: Capture potential interactions between features. Imagine creating a feature representing the product of two existing features to account for how they might influence each other.

_Dimensionality Reduction: When dealing with a high number of features, dimensionality reduction techniques can be essential. These techniques help reduce the complexity of your data while preserving the most important information. Here are two common approaches:

Principal Component Analysis (PCA): This popular technique transforms your features into a new set of uncorrelated features, prioritizing those with the most variance (informative ones).

Feature selection: This involves selecting a subset of the most relevant features from your original set. This can be achieved through various techniques like filter methods (based on statistical properties) or wrapper methods (based on model performance).

Feature Selection: Not all features are created equal. Feature selection techniques help identify the most relevant features that contribute the most to your model's learning process. This can not only improve model performance but also enhance interpretability by focusing on the features that truly matter. Here are some common selection methods:

Filter methods: These methods rank features based on a statistical measure of their correlation with the target variable (e.g., chi-square test, information gain). Features exceeding a certain threshold are selected.

Wrapper methods: These methods evaluate feature subsets based on the performance of a machine learning model trained on those features. Feature combinations that lead to the best model performance are selected.

By effectively applying these techniques, you can transform your raw data into a well-crafted set of features that empowers your machine learning models to achieve optimal performance. The next section will explore how Rag programming adds a unique twist to this essential process.

4.2 Rag Programming's Special Spices (with code examples)

Regular feature engineering techniques provide a solid foundation, but Rag programming injects a unique flavor that elevates the process to an art form. Here's how Rag programming adds its magic touch to feature engineering, along with code examples using Langchain:

Knowledge Base Integration:

Entity Linking with Langchain:

Python

```python
# (Placeholder code) Simulate entity linking with
Langchain
def link_entities_to_kb(data):
    # Use Langchain's Retriever library to link
entities in the 'product' column to a knowledge
base
                    linked_entities           =
langchain.retriever.link(data["product"],
kb_name="product_knowledge_base")
    # Extract relevant information from the linked
entities (e.g., product category, average rating)
    # ... (implementation details)
    # Update data with retrieved information
    # ... (implementation details)
    return data

# Example usage
data  =  pd.DataFrame({"product":  ["iPhone  13",
"Airpods Pro", "Samsung Galaxy S22"]})
data = link_entities_to_kb(data)
```

```
print(data)  # Dataframe with additional features
extracted from the knowledge base
```

External Data Augmentation:

Text Data Augmentation with Langchain:

Python

```python
# (Placeholder code) Simulate retrieving news
articles with Langchain
def retrieve_related_articles(data):
  # Use Langchain's Retriever library to retrieve
news articles related to topics in the 'text'
column
                        articles                =
langchain.retriever.text_search(data["text"],
external_source="news_api")
  # Process and analyze retrieved articles (e.g.,
sentiment analysis)
   # ... (implementation details)
    # Extract relevant information for feature
creation (e.g., overall sentiment score)
   # ... (implementation details)
  return data, additional_features

# Example usage
data = pd.DataFrame({"text": ["Great news! Apple
released the iPhone 13"]})
data,              sentiment_features              =
retrieve_related_articles(data)
print(data)  # Dataframe with the original text
```

```python
print(sentiment_features)  # Extracted sentiment
features from retrieved articles
```

Text Feature Engineering with External Knowledge:

Sentiment Lexicon Integration:

Python

```python
# Sample sentiment lexicon (positive and negative
words)
sentiment_lexicon  =  {"positive":  ["happy",
"good", "excellent"], "negative": ["sad", "bad",
"terrible"]}

def sentiment_feature_engineering(text):
  # Tokenize the text
  tokens = text.split()
    # Calculate sentiment scores based on the
lexicon
        positive_count  =  sum(token  in
sentiment_lexicon["positive"]  for  token  in
tokens)
        negative_count  =  sum(token  in
sentiment_lexicon["negative"]  for  token  in
tokens)
  return positive_count, negative_count

# Example usage
text = "The new movie was okay, but the acting
was a bit disappointing."
positive_count,         negative_count         =
sentiment_feature_engineering(text)
```

```
print(f"Positive     count:     {positive_count},
Negative count: {negative_count}")
```

These examples showcase how Langchain empowers you to leverage external knowledge and data sources during feature engineering in Rag programming. By incorporating these techniques, you can create feature sets that go beyond the limitations of your core data, unlocking the full potential of your machine learning models.

Note: These are simplified examples. In practice, you might need to handle potential errors from external sources, perform more advanced data processing on retrieved information, and integrate the retrieved data into your feature creation logic.

4.3 Crafting Features with Langchain:

Langchain plays a central role in Rag programming's feature engineering capabilities. By leveraging Langchain's Retriever library and its ability to access external knowledge sources, you can craft powerful and informative features for your machine learning models. Here's a deeper dive into how Langchain empowers feature engineering:

1. Retrieving Information for Feature Creation:

Concept Retrieval: Imagine you're working with a dataset containing product descriptions. A core feature might be the product name itself. However, Rag programming allows you to use Langchain to retrieve additional information about those products from external sources like product databases or e-commerce websites. This could include technical specifications, customer reviews, or average ratings. By incorporating this retrieved information, you can create new features that enrich your understanding of the products and potentially improve the performance of your models.

Python

```python
# (Placeholder code) Simulate retrieving product
information from an external database
def get_product_details(product_name):
  # Use Langchain's Retriever library to access a
product database
                        product_info              =
langchain.retriever.lookup(product_name,
external_source="product_database")
    # Extract relevant information for feature
creation (e.g., category, price, average rating)
  # ... (implementation details)
  return product_info

# Example usage
product_name = "iPhone 13"
product_details                                    =
get_product_details(product_name)
print(product_details)   # Dictionary containing
retrieved product information
```

_Text Retrieval for Feature Engineering: For tasks involving text data, Langchain allows you to retrieve relevant text snippets or documents from external sources. This can be particularly useful for:

Sentiment Analysis: Imagine you're analyzing customer reviews. By retrieving additional reviews or product descriptions related to the products mentioned, you can create more comprehensive features that capture the overall sentiment surrounding those products.

Topic Modeling: When working with large amounts of text data, topic modeling can be a powerful technique. Langchain allows you to retrieve documents that are thematically similar to the text in your data. This can be used to enrich your feature set by incorporating information about broader topics relevant to your data.

Python

```python
# (Placeholder code) Simulate retrieving related
documents with Langchain
def get_related_documents(text):
    # Use Langchain's Retriever library to find
similar documents from an external corpus
                related_documents          =
langchain.retriever.text_search(text,
external_source="document_corpus")
    # Process and analyze retrieved documents
(e.g., topic modeling)
  # ... (implementation details)
    # Extract relevant information for feature
creation (e.g., dominant topics)
  # ... (implementation details)
  return related_documents, additional_features

# Example usage
text = "This new movie is a sci-fi adventure with
a great storyline."
related_documents,        topic_features       =
get_related_documents(text)
print(related_documents)   # List of retrieved
documents
```

```
print(topic_features)  # Extracted topic features
based on retrieved documents
```

2. Entity Linking with Langchain:

Entity Enrichment: Entity linking involves identifying and linking entities within your data (like people, places, or organizations) to relevant entries in a knowledge base. This retrieved information can be a goldmine for feature engineering. Imagine a dataset containing news articles. By linking entities like named people or locations to a knowledge base, you can extract additional information about those entities, such as their profession, affiliation, or historical context. This information can then be used to create informative features for tasks like news article classification or information retrieval.

Python

```python
# (Placeholder code) Simulate entity linking with
Langchain
def link_entities_to_kb(text):
    # Use Langchain's Retriever library to link
entities in the text to a knowledge base
                    linked_entities            =
langchain.retriever.link(text,
kb_name="general_knowledge_base")
    # Extract relevant information from the linked
entities (e.g., entity type, description)
    # ... (implementation details)
      # Update features based on retrieved
information
    # ... (implementation details)
    return linked_entities, updated_features

# Example usage
```

```
text = "The president visited Paris yesterday."
linked_entities,        entity_features        =
link_entities_to_kb(text)
print(linked_entities)   # Dictionary containing
information about linked entities
print(entity_features)   # Features enriched with
entity information
```

By leveraging these Langchain functionalities, you can transform
your feature engineering process from basic data manipulation to
a knowledge-infused exploration that creates a richer and more
informative foundation for your machine

4.4 Beyond the Recipe: Experimentation and Optimization

Feature engineering is an iterative and experimental process. While Rag programming with Langchain provides powerful tools, there's no single "best" recipe for crafting features that guarantees success for every machine learning task. This section highlights the importance of experimentation and optimization to identify the most effective feature sets for your models.

The Art of Exploration:

Trying Different Techniques: Don't be afraid to experiment with various feature creation, dimensionality reduction, and feature selection techniques. Explore different approaches and evaluate their impact on your model's performance.

Understanding the Data: Gain a deep understanding of the data you're working with. This includes exploring data distributions, identifying potential relationships between features, and understanding the inherent characteristics of the data that might influence feature engineering decisions.

Domain Knowledge is Key: Incorporate your knowledge of the specific problem domain you're tackling. This can guide you in selecting features that are likely to be most relevant to the task and help you identify potential external knowledge sources that Langchain can exploit.

Using Langchain for Feature Exploration:

Langchain's capabilities can aid your experimentation process in feature engineering:

Rapid Prototyping: Quickly test different feature engineering ideas using Langchain. Its ability to interact with external sources allows you to experiment with incorporating various knowledge sources and data augmentations into your feature creation process.

Iterative Refinement: The modular nature of Langchain makes it easy to refine your feature engineering pipeline. You can isolate specific feature creation steps and experiment with different options within Langchain's framework.

Optimizing Feature Performance:

Evaluation Metrics: Use appropriate evaluation metrics to assess the effectiveness of your feature set. This might involve metrics like accuracy, precision, recall, or F1-score depending on your specific machine learning task.

Feature Importance Analysis: Techniques like feature importance analysis can help you understand which features contribute most to your model's performance. This can guide you in refining your feature set by focusing on the most impactful features and potentially removing redundant ones.

Model Selection and Tuning: The effectiveness of your feature set can also be influenced by the choice of machine learning model and its hyperparameters. Experiment with different models and tuning techniques to identify the best fit for your feature set.

By continuously experimenting, evaluating, and refining your feature engineering approach, you can ensure that your machine learning models have the strongest possible foundation for success. Here's a glimpse into the exciting world of Rag programming applications in the next chapter.

#### Chapter 5:

Machine Learning Masterpieces: Building Powerful Models with Rag Programming

Congratulations! You've mastered the art of feature engineering with Rag programming, transforming raw data into informative features that empower your machine learning models. This chapter delves into the exciting world of building powerful models using Rag programming. Here, we'll explore how Rag programming seamlessly integrates with various machine learning algorithms, allowing you to create state-of-the-art solutions for a wide range of tasks.

The Rag Programming Workflow:

Rag programming follows a structured workflow that leverages its strengths for building robust machine learning models:

1. **Data Preparation:** This stage involves data cleaning, wrangling, and transformation using the techniques explored in Chapter 3. Rag programming integrates seamlessly with tools like Pandas for data manipulation and Langchain for incorporating external knowledge sources.
2. **Feature Engineering:** Chapter 4 equipped you with the skills to craft informative features from your data. Rag programming empowers you to go beyond traditional techniques by leveraging external knowledge bases and data sources through Langchain.
3. **Model Selection and Training:** This stage involves choosing a suitable machine learning algorithm for your

specific task. Rag programming is agnostic to the choice of model, allowing you to leverage various algorithms from libraries like scikit-learn or TensorFlow.

4. **Model Evaluation and Refinement:** Evaluate your model's performance using appropriate metrics and techniques. Rag programming allows you to analyze feature importance and fine-tune your model for optimal performance.

The Rag Programming Advantage:

While traditional machine learning pipelines can be effective, Rag programming offers several advantages:

- **Knowledge-Infused Models:** By incorporating external knowledge through Langchain, Rag programming enables you to build models that are not only data-driven but also contextually aware. This can lead to significant improvements in performance, especially for complex tasks.
- **Flexible Feature Engineering:** Rag programming empowers you to explore various feature engineering approaches and leverage external data sources. This flexibility allows you to create richer feature sets that capture a more comprehensive understanding of the problem domain.
- **Rapid Prototyping and Experimentation:** Langchain's capabilities facilitate rapid prototyping of feature engineering ideas and experimentation with different knowledge sources. This allows you to iterate quickly and identify the most effective model configurations.

Rag Programming in Action: Examples

Here are some examples of how Rag programming can be applied to build powerful machine learning models:

- **Sentiment Analysis with Knowledge Bases:** Imagine analyzing customer reviews to understand sentiment towards a product. Rag programming allows you to link product entities to knowledge bases containing information about product specifications or customer ratings. This enriched feature set can lead to more accurate sentiment analysis.
- **Recommender Systems with External Knowledge:** A recommender system might traditionally rely on user behavior data. Rag programming allows you to incorporate external knowledge about product features, user demographics, or even social media trends to create more personalized and relevant recommendations.
- **Question Answering with Enhanced Context:** A question-answering system can benefit from Rag programming's ability to access external knowledge sources like knowledge bases or factual documents. By providing additional context to the model, Rag programming can improve the accuracy and informativeness of the answers provided.

Beyond the Examples:

The potential applications of Rag programming in machine learning are vast and constantly evolving. As you explore this powerful approach, keep these key takeaways in mind:

- **Focus on the Problem Domain:** Understanding the specific task and the data you're working with is crucial. This knowledge guides you in selecting appropriate algorithms and leveraging Rag programming's strengths effectively.

- **Experimentation is Key:** Don't be afraid to experiment with different feature engineering techniques, knowledge sources, and model configurations. Rag programming's flexibility empowers you to explore various options and identify the best fit for your needs.
- **Stay Curious and Explore:** The field of machine learning is constantly evolving, and Rag programming is at the forefront of this innovation. Stay up-to-date with the latest advancements and explore how Rag programming can push the boundaries of what's possible in your machine learning projects.

By mastering the concepts and techniques presented in this chapter, you are well-equipped to leverage Rag programming's capabilities to build powerful and knowledge-infused machine learning models. Remember, the journey of exploration and discovery in the world of Rag programming has just begun!

5.1 Bringing in the Best: Integrating Popular Machine Learning Libraries

Rag programming's magic lies in its ability to seamlessly integrate with various machine learning libraries. This empowers you to leverage the strengths of established frameworks while incorporating the unique advantages of Rag programming's knowledge-infused approach. Here, we'll delve into how Rag programming plays nicely with some of the most popular machine learning libraries:

Scikit-learn:

A Perfect Match: Scikit-learn is a widely used library known for its comprehensive suite of classical machine learning algorithms. Rag programming integrates smoothly with scikit-learn, allowing you to leverage its algorithms (e.g., linear regression, decision trees, support vector machines) within your Rag programming workflow.

Workflow Integration: After preparing your data and crafting informative features using Rag programming's techniques, you can seamlessly pass your features to scikit-learn for model training and evaluation. Scikit-learn's familiar syntax and vast array of algorithms make it a natural fit for building various machine learning models within a Rag programming pipeline.

Python

```python
# Example: Rag programming with scikit-learn for
sentiment analysis

# (Assuming you have sentiment features created
using Rag programming)
from            sklearn.linear_model            import
LogisticRegression

# Train a logistic regression model for sentiment
classification
model = LogisticRegression()
model.fit(X_train,   y_train)      #   X_train   and
y_train are your training features and labels

# Use the trained model for sentiment prediction
predictions = model.predict(X_test)

# Evaluate model performance using appropriate
metrics
```

TensorFlow and PyTorch:

Deep Learning Powerhouses: TensorFlow and PyTorch are dominant frameworks for deep learning applications. Rag programming integrates effectively with these frameworks, allowing you to leverage their capabilities for building complex neural network architectures.

Knowledge Infusion with Deep Learning: While TensorFlow and PyTorch excel at deep learning, Rag programming adds an extra layer of power. Imagine a scenario where you're building a deep learning model for image classification. Rag programming allows you to retrieve additional information about the images (e.g., object descriptions from a knowledge base) and incorporate this information into your model's training process. This can lead to improved performance and more robust models.

Python

```python
# (Placeholder code) Simulate retrieving image
descriptions with Langchain
def get_image_descriptions(image_urls):
  # Use Langchain's Retriever library to access
an image recognition API
                    descriptions                =
langchain.retriever.text_search(image_urls,
external_source="image_recognition_api")
  # Process and format retrieved descriptions for
deep learning model
  # ... (implementation details)
  return descriptions


# Integrate retrieved descriptions into your
TensorFlow/PyTorch model for image classification
# ... (implementation details)
```

Beyond the Usual Suspects:

The world of machine learning libraries is vast, and Rag programming is not limited to the ones mentioned above. Here are some additional points to consider:

Compatibility: When choosing a library, ensure compatibility with your preferred programming language (Python in most cases) and check if there are any known integration issues with Rag programming or Langchain.

Task-Specific Libraries: For specialized tasks like natural language processing or computer vision, explore libraries specifically designed for those domains. Rag programming can still play a crucial role in feature engineering and knowledge integration within these workflows.

By understanding how Rag programming interacts with popular machine learning libraries, you can leverage the strengths of both worlds to build powerful and effective models. Remember, the choice of library ultimately depends on the specific needs of your machine learning project.

The next section will explore how Rag programming empowers you to continuously improve your models through ongoing learning and adaptation.

5.2 Perfecting Your Dish: Streamlining Model Training and Evaluation (with code examples)

Just like a seasoned chef refines a dish based on feedback, Rag programming empowers you to continuously improve your machine learning models through streamlined training and evaluation processes. This section explores techniques with code examples to ensure your models reach their full potential.

Efficient Training with Langchain:

Parallelization for Scalability (placeholder code):

Python

```python
# (Placeholder code) Simulate parallel training
with Langchain
def parallel_train_model(model, X_train, y_train,
num_workers):
    # Divide data into batches and distribute
training tasks across multiple workers
(processes/machines) using Langchain's
parallelization functionalities
  # ... (implementation details)
  # Aggregate training results from all workers
and update the model
  # ... (implementation details)
  return model


# Example usage (assuming you have a training
function for your machine learning model)
model = train_model(X_train, y_train)  # Regular
training
parallel_model = parallel_train_model(model,
X_train, y_train, num_workers=4)
```

Lazy Evaluation for Resource Optimization (placeholder code):

Python

```python
# (Placeholder code) Simulate lazy evaluation
with Langchain
def       train_model_with_lazy_evaluation(model,
X_train, y_train):
  # Use Langchain's lazy evaluation capabilities
to defer data retrieval and processing until it's
needed during training
  # ... (implementation details)
  # Train the model with optimized data access
patterns
  # ... (implementation details)
  return model

# Example usage
model = train_model_with_lazy_evaluation(model,
X_train, y_train)
```

Leveraging Active Learning (placeholder code):

Python

```python
# (Placeholder code) Simulate active learning
with Langchain
def   active_learning(model,   X_pool,   y_pool,
uncertainty_sampling_strategy):
  # Use an active learning framework to select
the most informative data points from the pool
(X_pool,    y_pool)    based    on    the
uncertainty_sampling_strategy
  # Leverage Langchain to retrieve those specific
data points for the model to learn from
  # ... (implementation details)
  # Update the model with the retrieved data
points
  # ... (implementation details)
```

```
    return model, updated_pool

# Example usage
uncertainty_sampling_strategy  =  "entropy"   #
Example strategy
model,  X_pool_updated  =  active_learning(model,
X_pool, y_pool, uncertainty_sampling_strategy)
```

Advanced Evaluation Techniques:

Error Analysis with Langchain (placeholder code):

Python

```
# (Placeholder code) Simulate error analysis with
Langchain
def analyze_errors(model, X_test, y_test):
    # Identify data points where the model made
errors
    # Leverage Langchain to retrieve additional
information (e.g., from knowledge bases) about
these specific data points
    # ... (implementation details)
    # Analyze the retrieved information to
understand the potential causes of errors
    # ... (implementation details)
    return error_analysis_report

# Example usage
error_analysis_report   =   analyze_errors(model,
X_test, y_test)
```

Continuous Learning and Improvement:

Model Monitoring with Langchain (placeholder code):

Python

```python
# (Placeholder code) Simulate model monitoring
with Langchain
def monitor_model_performance(model, new_data,
new_labels):
  # Evaluate the model's performance on the new
data using Langchain to retrieve and process the
data efficiently
  # ... (implementation details)
   # Track performance metrics over time and
identify potential degradation
  # ... (implementation details)
  return performance_report

# Example usage
performance_report                              =
monitor_model_performance(model,        new_data,
new_labels)
```

Adaptive Learning with Refreshed Knowledge (placeholder code):

Python

```python
# (Placeholder code) Simulate adaptive learning
with Langchain
def
update_knowledge_sources(knowledge_base_name):
   # Use Langchain to access external APIs or
databases to update the information within the
specified knowledge base
  # ... (implementation details)
```

```
    return updated_knowledge_base

# Example usage
updated_kb                                              =
update_knowledge_sources(knowledge_base_name="pro
duct_information")

# During training, use the updated knowledge base
for feature creation or model adaptation
# ... (implementation details)
```

By incorporating these techniques, you can transform the model training and evaluation process from a static procedure to a dynamic cycle of learning and improvement. This

5.3 Tuning for Peak Flavor: Hyperparameter Tuning for Optimal Performance with Rag Programming

Hyperparameter tuning is a crucial aspect of machine learning that involves adjusting the settings of your model to achieve the best possible performance. Rag programming, with its unique blend of feature engineering and knowledge integration, introduces additional layers to consider during hyperparameter tuning. Here's how to effectively tune your Rag programming models for peak performance:

Tuning Traditional Hyperparameters:

The Usual Suspects: Don't neglect the standard hyperparameters associated with your chosen machine learning algorithm (e.g., learning rate for gradient descent, number of trees in a random forest). Utilize techniques like grid search or random search to explore different configurations and identify the settings that lead to optimal performance on your specific task.

Integration with Langchain: While tuning traditional hyperparameters, keep in mind how Langchain interacts with your model. For instance, if you're using lazy evaluation, consider how it might affect the training process at different hyperparameter settings.

Tuning Feature Engineering Hyperparameters:

Feature Selection: The effectiveness of your feature set significantly impacts model performance. Techniques like L1 or L2 regularization can be used to penalize models for using too many features, leading to the selection of a more optimal subset.

Knowledge Source Parameters: When incorporating external knowledge sources through Langchain, you might have additional hyperparameters to consider. For example, imagine using a knowledge base with different confidence scores for retrieved information. Tuning a threshold for selecting information based on these confidence scores could be a hyperparameter to explore.

Co-Tuning for Optimal Performance:

Traditionally, hyperparameter tuning often treats feature engineering and model parameters as separate entities. Rag programming encourages a more holistic approach:

Co-dependent Parameters: Recognize that feature engineering choices using Langchain and traditional model hyperparameters can be interdependent. For instance, the optimal number of features might be influenced by the learning algorithm and its specific hyperparameter settings.

Grid Search with Feature Engineering: Consider expanding your grid search or random search to include not just traditional model hyperparameters but also variations in your feature engineering pipeline. This allows you to explore the combined effect of both sets of parameters on your model's performance.

Leveraging Langchain for Efficiency:

Parallelization for Faster Tuning: Langchain's parallelization capabilities can be a valuable asset during hyperparameter tuning. By distributing evaluation tasks across multiple cores or machines, you can explore different hyperparameter configurations more efficiently.

Lazy Evaluation for Resource Management: Lazy evaluation with Langchain can help optimize resource usage during hyperparameter tuning, especially when dealing with large datasets or complex feature engineering workflows.

By adopting these strategies, you can effectively navigate the hyperparameter tuning landscape within Rag programming. Remember, the goal is to find the configuration that allows your model to learn the most from the data and external knowledge, ultimately achieving the best possible performance on your target task.

The next chapter will delve into the exciting world of real-world applications where Rag programming can unleash its full potential.

1. **Content Shift:** We can keep the chapter title (Chapter 6: Advanced Rag Programming Techniques: Optimizing Your Model) but shift the content to focus on advanced techniques that go beyond hyperparameter tuning. Here are some potential areas to explore:

   o **Ensemble Learning with Rag Programming:** Explore how Rag programming can be used to create ensemble models that combine the strengths of different machine learning algorithms. This could involve using Langchain to generate diverse feature sets for each model in the ensemble.

   o **Transfer Learning with External Knowledge:** Discuss how Rag programming can leverage pre-trained models and external knowledge bases to improve the performance of models on new tasks. This could involve using knowledge graphs to identify similarities between tasks and fine-tune pre-trained models for specific use cases.

   o **Explainable AI (XAI) with Rag Programming:** Explore how Rag programming can be used to make machine learning models more interpretable. This could involve using Langchain to trace a model's decision-making process back to the specific pieces of knowledge or data points that influenced its predictions.

By incorporating these suggestions, you can provide a more comprehensive exploration of advanced Rag programming techniques that go beyond hyperparameter tuning and showcase its capabilities in real-world applications.

6.1 Automating the Selection Process: Automating Model Selection with Rag Programming

In the realm of Rag programming, where knowledge infusion and feature engineering reign supreme, the task of model selection can become more nuanced. Traditional approaches that rely solely on data characteristics might not capture the full potential of Rag programming's ability to leverage external knowledge. This chapter explores strategies for automating model selection within the Rag programming framework, ensuring your models are well-equipped to harness the power of both data and knowledge.

Challenges of Traditional Model Selection:

Limited Data Focus: Conventional methods often primarily consider intrinsic data properties (size, distribution, etc.) when selecting a model. Rag programming introduces an additional layer of complexity, as external knowledge sources can significantly influence model performance.

Knowledge Integration Impact: The effectiveness of different machine learning algorithms can vary depending on how Rag programming integrates external knowledge into the feature engineering process.

Automating Model Selection with Rag Programming (without code examples):

While providing specific code examples for automating model selection with Rag programming can be challenging due to the evolving nature of libraries and the absence of a standardized approach, here are the key concepts and reasoning behind potential strategies:

1. Meta-Learning for Informed Decisions:

Concept: Meta-learning algorithms can learn from past Rag programming projects to suggest promising models for new tasks. They analyze data characteristics, knowledge sources used, and model performances from previous projects.

Reasoning: By leveraging past experiences, meta-learning can provide a more informed starting point for model selection in new projects, especially when dealing with similar data and knowledge domains.

2. Automated Feature Engineering Exploration:

Concept: Techniques like automated feature selection or hyperparameter tuning can be used to explore various feature sets and their impact on different machine learning algorithms. This exploration can be automated to identify the combination of model and feature engineering that yields the best performance.

Reasoning: Automating feature engineering exploration allows for the evaluation of a wider range of feature combinations and their interaction with different models. This can help identify unexpected high performers or uncover feature engineering approaches that are particularly effective when combined with specific knowledge sources.

3. Knowledge-Aware Model Selection:

Concept: Move beyond pure data-driven decision-making. Integrate information about the external knowledge sources being used into the model selection process. For instance, if a project heavily relies on a knowledge base with rich semantic relationships, models adept at handling such relationships (e.g., graph neural networks) might be prioritized as candidates.

Reasoning: By considering the characteristics of the knowledge sources, you can make more informed choices about the types of models that are likely to benefit most from the infused knowledge. This can lead to a more targeted and effective selection process.

A Hybrid Approach: Combining Automation and Human Expertise

While automation offers efficiency, human expertise remains crucial. Here's a two-step approach:

Leverage Automation: Utilize meta-learning and automated feature engineering exploration to generate a shortlist of promising models based on your data, knowledge sources, and past project experiences.

Human Oversight and Refinement: Subject the shortlisted models to further evaluation with domain-specific knowledge and considerations. This might involve factors like interpretability requirements, computational resource constraints, or the need for online learning capabilities.

Benefits of Automating Model Selection with Rag Programming:

Improved Efficiency: Automating repetitive tasks like feature engineering exploration frees up time for data scientists to focus on higher-level aspects like knowledge source integration and model interpretation

Reduced Bias: Automated selection methods can help mitigate the potential for bias that can creep into human decision-making during model selection.

Exploration of a Wider Range of Models: Automation allows for the evaluation of a broader set of models than might be feasible with manual selection, potentially leading to the discovery of unexpected high performers.

Remember: Automation is a powerful tool, but it's not a silver bullet. Combining it with human expertise ensures a well-rounded and effective model selection process within the Rag programming framework.

The Road Ahead:

The field of automated model selection with Rag programming is an active area of research. Future advancements may involve:

Advanced Meta-Learning Techniques: The development of more sophisticated meta-learning algorithms that can not only suggest models but also provide guidance on hyperparameter tuning and feature engineering specific to Rag programming workflows.

Explainable AI (XAI) for Model Selection: Integrating XAI techniques into the selection process to understand the rationale behind the automated recommendations and provide insights into the relationship between knowledge sources, feature engineering, and model performance.

By embracing automation while maintaining human oversight, you can ensure that your Rag programming projects leverage the best

6.2 Combining Strengths: Ensemble Learning and Stacking Techniques with Rag Programming

Rag programming's ability to harness external knowledge through Langchain opens doors for powerful ensemble learning approaches. This chapter explores how ensemble learning techniques, particularly stacking, can be leveraged within Rag programming to create even more robust and effective machine learning models.

_Ensemble Learning: A Synergy of Models

Ensemble learning combines predictions from multiple models to create a single, often more accurate prediction. This approach leverages the strengths of different models, potentially reducing variance and improving overall performance. Here's how Rag programming integrates seamlessly with ensemble methods:

Knowledge-Infused Base Learners: Each individual model (base learner) within the ensemble can benefit from Rag programming's feature engineering capabilities. By incorporating knowledge from external sources, you can create more informative features for each base learner, potentially leading to stronger individual models.

Diversity through Feature Engineering: Rag programming allows you to explore various feature engineering approaches for each base learner. This can help create a more diverse ensemble, where individual models make predictions based on different aspects of the data and knowledge.

_Stacking: A Powerful Ensemble Technique

Stacking, a particular type of ensemble learning, involves training a meta-model to learn how to combine the predictions from multiple base learners. Here's how Rag programming enhances stacking:

Knowledge-Infused Meta-Learner: The meta-model in stacking can also leverage Rag programming for feature engineering. Imagine a scenario where you use base learners that analyze different aspects of text data (e.g., sentiment analysis, topic modeling). Rag programming can allow the meta-model to access knowledge sources like sentiment lexicons or topic hierarchies to create additional features that inform its combination of the base learner predictions.

Leveraging Rag Programming for Stacking:

Prepare Data and Knowledge Sources: Preprocess your data and identify relevant knowledge sources that can be used for feature engineering throughout the ensemble creation process.

Train Base Learners: Train multiple base learners using Rag programming for feature engineering. You can experiment with different machine learning algorithms and feature engineering approaches for each base learner.

Generate Base Learner Predictions: Once trained, use the base learners to generate predictions on a held-out validation set.

Create Meta-Learner Features: Employ Rag programming to create informative features for the meta-model. These features can include the base learner predictions, as well as additional knowledge-infused features derived from external sources.

Train the Meta-Learner: Train the meta-model using the base learner predictions and the additional features created with Rag programming.

Make Final Predictions: Use the trained meta-model to make final predictions on new data by combining the predictions from the base learners.

Benefits of Stacking with Rag Programming:

Improved Model Performance: By leveraging knowledge-infused base learners and a meta-learner that can exploit this knowledge, stacking with Rag programming can lead to more accurate and robust models.

Reduced Variance: The ensemble approach helps to reduce the variance of individual models, leading to more consistent predictions.

Flexibility in Base Learner Choice: Rag programming allows you to experiment with various machine learning algorithms for the base learners, leveraging their strengths and tailoring them to specific knowledge sources.

Remember: While stacking offers advantages, it can also introduce additional complexity. Carefully consider the trade-off between potential performance gains and the increased training time and computational resources required for building and training an ensemble.

The next chapter will delve into real-world applications where Rag programming and ensemble learning techniques can be harnessed to solve challenging problems.

6.3 Distributed Dining: Leveraging Langchain for Distributed Training and Optimization

In the fast-paced world of machine learning, training models on massive datasets can be a time-consuming endeavor. Rag programming, with its knowledge integration capabilities, can further amplify the computational demands. This chapter explores how Langchain, Rag programming's companion library, empowers you with distributed training and optimization techniques to tackle large-scale machine learning projects efficiently.

_The Challenge of Scalability:

Data Deluge: Modern datasets can reach enormous sizes, posing challenges for traditional training methods on a single machine. Training times can become excessive, hindering the development process.

Resource Constraints: Limited computational resources on a single machine might restrict the complexity of models you can train or the size of datasets you can handle effectively.

_Langchain to the Rescue: Distributed Training with Rag Programming

Langchain's distributed training capabilities allow you to leverage multiple machines or cores to accelerate the training process for Rag programming models. Here's how it breaks down:

Parallelization Power: Langchain can distribute training tasks across multiple machines or cores within a cluster. This parallelization approach significantly reduces training times, especially for computationally expensive models or large datasets.

Efficient Knowledge Access: Langchain's distributed architecture ensures efficient retrieval and processing of knowledge sources even in a distributed training setting. This is crucial, as Rag programming relies heavily on external knowledge for feature engineering.

Distributed Training with Langchain (placeholder code):

Python

```python
#  (Placeholder  code)  Simulate  distributed
training with Langchain
def    train_model_distributed(model,    X_train,
y_train, num_workers):
   # Split data and knowledge source access among
worker processes
   # Leverage Langchain's distributed capabilities
to  train  the  model  in  parallel  across  multiple
workers
   # ... (implementation details)
   # Aggregate training results from all workers
and update the model
   # ... (implementation details)
   return model
```

```
# Example usage (assuming you have a training
function for your machine learning model)
model = train_model(X_train, y_train)  # Regular
training
parallel_model  =  train_model_distributed(model,
X_train, y_train, num_workers=4)
```

Optimizing the Feast: Hyperparameter Tuning at Scale

Distributed Hyperparameter Search: Langchain's capabilities extend beyond training. You can leverage its distributed architecture to perform hyperparameter tuning more efficiently. By evaluating different hyperparameter configurations on multiple machines simultaneously, you can significantly reduce the time it takes to find the optimal settings for your Rag programming model.

Scalable Resource Allocation: With distributed training, you can allocate resources more effectively. By dynamically assigning workloads based on machine availability, Langchain helps ensure that your computational resources are utilized efficiently throughout the training and optimization process.

The Benefits of Distributed Training and Optimization:

Reduced Training Times: By distributing the workload across multiple machines, Langchain can significantly accelerate the training process for Rag programming models, allowing you to experiment more rapidly and iterate faster.

Handling Larger Datasets: Distributed training allows you to tackle datasets that would be impractical to handle on a single machine. This opens doors to working with richer and more comprehensive data sources, potentially leading to improved model performance.

Efficient Resource Utilization: Langchain optimizes resource allocation during training and hyperparameter tuning, ensuring you get the most out of your computational resources.

_Beyond Distribution: The Future of Scalable Rag Programming

The field of distributed training and optimization is constantly evolving. Here are some exciting possibilities on the horizon:

Cloud-Based Training: Leverage cloud platforms that offer scalable compute resources to further accelerate training times for large-scale Rag programming models.

Integration with AutoML Tools: Explore the potential of combining Langchain's distributed training capabilities with automated machine learning (AutoML) tools to streamline the hyperparameter tuning process for Rag programming workflows.

By adopting distributed training and optimization techniques with Langchain, you can empower your Rag programming projects to handle ever-growing datasets and complex models, ultimately unlocking the full potential of knowledge-infused machine learning.

Chapter 7:

Deep Learning Delicacies: Building Deep Neural Networks with Rag Programming

Rag programming's ability to integrate external knowledge opens doors to exciting applications in the realm of deep learning. This chapter explores how Rag programming can be used to create and enhance deep neural networks (DNNs), empowering you to leverage the power of both data and knowledge for complex tasks.

DNNs and Knowledge Infusion:

- **Traditional Deep Learning:** Deep learning excels at pattern recognition and feature extraction from raw data. However, it often requires vast amounts of data to achieve optimal performance.

-
- **Knowledge as a Guiding Light:** Rag programming injects knowledge from external sources to guide the learning process of DNNs. This can be particularly beneficial for tasks where data might be limited or noisy.

-

Synergistic Approaches:

Here's how Rag programming and deep learning can be combined to create effective models:

1. **Knowledge-Infused Feature Engineering:** Before feeding data into a DNN, leverage Rag programming to extract informative features that incorporate knowledge from

external sources. This can significantly improve the quality of the input data for the DNN.
2. **Knowledge-Enhanced Network Architectures:** Explore DNN architectures specifically designed to handle knowledge infusion. This could involve incorporating knowledge graphs or symbolic reasoning techniques into the network structure.
3. **Regularization with External Knowledge:** Regularization techniques are often used to prevent DNNs from overfitting on training data. Rag programming allows you to introduce knowledge-based regularization terms that can further improve modelgeneralizability.

Leveraging Langchain for DNNs:

- **Scalable Knowledge Access:** Langchain's distributed capabilities ensure efficient retrieval and processing of knowledge sources, even when working with large DNNs that require substantial amounts of data and external information.
- **Integration with Deep Learning Frameworks:** Rag programming can be seamlessly integrated with popular deep learning frameworks like TensorFlow or PyTorch. This allows you to leverage the strengths of both frameworks, using Rag programming for feature engineering and knowledge integration, and the deep learning frameworks for model building and training.
-

Example: Knowledge-Infused Text Classification with DNNs

Imagine a scenario where you want to build a DNN to classify news articles into different categories (e.g., politics, sports, business). Here's how Rag programming can enhance the process:

1. **Feature Engineering with Knowledge:** Use Rag programming to extract features from the text data, such as named entity recognition or topic modeling. Additionally, leverage knowledge bases to identify relevant entities and their relationships.
2. **DNN for Text Classification:** Build a DNN that takes the extracted features and knowledge-infused information as input. The DNN can then learn to classify news articles based on the combined information.

Benefits of Deep Learning with Rag Programming:

- **Improved Performance:** By incorporating knowledge, you can potentially improve the accuracy andgeneralizability of deep learning models, especially when dealing with limited or noisy data.
- **Interpretability with Knowledge:** Knowledge infusion can aid in explaining the DNN's decision-making process. By tracing how the model uses external knowledge, you can gain insights into its reasoning patterns.
- **Reduced Data Reliance:** Knowledge integration can alleviate the need for massive datasets, making deep learning more accessible for tasks with limited data availability.

Challenges and Considerations:

- **Model Complexity:** Deep learning models with knowledge infusion can become more complex, requiring careful design and potentially more computational resources for training.

- **Data Alignment:** Ensure that the data used for training the DNN and the knowledge sources are aligned and consistent to avoid introducing contradictions or biases.

The Future of Deep Learning with Rag Programming

The field of deep learning with knowledge infusion is continuously evolving. Here are some exciting possibilities to explore:

- **Attention Mechanisms with Knowledge Graphs:** Investigate how attention mechanisms in DNNs can be adapted to focus on specific parts of the knowledge graph that are most relevant to the task at hand.

-
- **Lifelong Learning with Continuously Updated Knowledge:** Explore how to develop DNNs that can continuously learn and adapt as new knowledge is incorporated from external sources.

-

By combining the power of deep learning with the knowledge integration capabilities of Rag programming, you can create robust and versatile models that excel at solving complex tasks, even in data-scarce environments.

7.1 Constructing the Masterpiece: Building and Training Deep Neural Networks with Python (Rag Programming + Deep Learning)

1. Environment Setup:

Install Python (version 3.6 or later recommended).

Install essential libraries:

`rag` (for Rag programming functionalities)

`tensorflow` or `pytorch` (popular deep learning frameworks) - We'll use TensorFlow for this example.

`numpy` (numerical computing library)

`pandas` (data manipulation library)

Depending on your chosen knowledge source, you might need additional libraries (e.g., library for accessing a specific knowledge base).

2. Data Preparation (placeholder code):

Python

```python
import pandas as pd

# Load your text data (replace 'your_data.csv'
with your actual file)
data = pd.read_csv("your_data.csv")

# Preprocess the text data (e.g., tokenization,
removal of stop words)
#    ...    (implementation    details    for    text
preprocessing)
```

3. Knowledge Source Integration with Rag Programming (placeholder code):

Python

```python
from rag import knowledge_graph

# Access your external knowledge source (replace
with your specific approach)
kg   =   knowledge_graph.KnowledgeGraph(...)        #
Replace "..." with connection details

# Example: Extract relevant entities from the
text data and link them to the knowledge graph
entities = []
for text in data["text"]:
  # Identify named entities in the text
  extracted_entities = identify_entities(text)
    # Link entities to knowledge graph entries
using Rag programming functions
  linked_entities = []
  for entity in extracted_entities:
    linked_entities.append(kg.search(entity))
  entities.append(linked_entities)

# Add linked entities as a new column to the
DataFrame
data["linked_entities"] = entities
```

4. Feature Engineering with Rag Programming (placeholder code):

Python

```python
from rag import feature_engineering
```

```python
# Extract word-level features (e.g., word
embeddings)
word_embeddings                              =
feature_engineering.word_embedding(data["text"])

# Leverage Rag programming to incorporate
knowledge-infused features
# Example: Use linked entities to create topic
features
topic_features                               =
feature_engineering.topic_modeling(data["text"],
data["linked_entities"])

# Combine word-level and knowledge-infused
features
combined_features                            =
np.concatenate((word_embeddings, topic_features),
axis=1)
```

5. Deep Neural Network Construction (placeholder code):

Python

```python
from tensorflow.keras.models import Sequential
from tensorflow.keras.layers import Dense,
Embedding

# Define the DNN architecture
model = Sequential()
model.add(Embedding(vocab_size, embedding_dim,
input_length=max_length))  # Input layer for text
model.add(Dense(units=128, activation="relu"))  #
Hidden layer
```

```python
model.add(Dense(num_classes,
activation="softmax"))      #  Output   layer   for
classification

# Compile the model
model.compile(loss="categorical_crossentropy",
optimizer="adam", metrics=["accuracy"])
```

6. Model Training (placeholder code):

Python

```python
from        sklearn.model_selection        import
train_test_split

# Split data into training, validation, and test
sets
X_train,    X_test,    y_train,    y_test    =
train_test_split(combined_features,
data["label"], test_size=0.2)

# Train the DNN model
model.fit(X_train,        y_train,        epochs=10,
validation_data=(X_test, y_test))
```

7. Evaluation and Refinement:

Evaluate the model's performance on the test set using appropriate metrics (e.g., accuracy, F1-score).

Analyze the results and refine the model if necessary (e.g., adjusting hyperparameters, experimenting with different DNN architectures, incorporating additional knowledge sources).

Key Considerations:

Data Alignment: Ensure consistency between the data used for training the DNN and the information retrieved from the knowledge source.

Model Complexity: Balance model complexity with available computational resources and the amount of data at hand.

Interpretability: Explore techniques to understand how the DNN leverages the knowledge infusion during the decision-making process

7.2 Efficient Workflows: Rag Programming Techniques for Efficient Deep Learning Workflows

1. Parallelized Text Preprocessing (placeholder code):

Python

```python
import    dask        #    Example    library    for
parallelization

# Load your text data
text_data = ...

def preprocess_text(text):
    #  Implement  your  text  preprocessing  steps
(e.g., tokenization, removal of stop words)
  # ...
    return preprocessed_text

# Parallelize preprocessing using dask
```

```
preprocessed_data                                =
dask.compute(dask.delayed(preprocess_text)(text)
for text in text_data)
```

2. Modular Feature Engineering Pipelines (placeholder code):

Python

```
from rag import feature_engineering

# Define functions for individual feature
engineering steps
def word_embedding_feature(text):
  # Implement word embedding generation
  # ...
  return embedding

def              knowledge_infused_feature(text,
knowledge_graph):
   # Extract knowledge-based features using the
knowledge graph
  # ...
  return knowledge_features

# Combine features from different modules
def              create_combined_features(text,
knowledge_graph):
  word_embeddings = word_embedding_feature(text)
                 knowledge_features            =
knowledge_infused_feature(text, knowledge_graph)
      return   np.concatenate((word_embeddings,
knowledge_features))

# Use the combined feature function in your
workflow
```

```
combined_features                              =
[create_combined_features(text,    knowledge_graph)
for text in text_data]
```

3. Automated Feature Selection (placeholder code):

Python

```
from        sklearn.feature_selection        import
SelectFromModel

# Train a model (e.g., logistic regression) to
identify important features
model = ...  # Train your model
selector = SelectFromModel(model, prefit=True)

# Select the most relevant features
selected_features                              =
selector.transform(combined_features)
```

4. Integration with AutoML Tools:

Explore libraries like `autokeras` or `TPOT` for automated hyperparameter tuning in deep learning models.

Integrate these libraries with your Rag programming workflow to automate both Rag programming and deep learning hyperparameter optimization.

5. Workflow Optimization Strategies:

Implement early stopping and model checkpointing techniques within your deep learning framework (e.g., TensorFlow, PyTorch).

Consider using Langchain's distributed training capabilities for large datasets or complex models (code example not provided due to library-specific implementation details).

Remember: This is a general guide, and specific implementations will vary depending on your chosen libraries and deep learning framework. Refer to the official documentation for detailed instructions and code examples.

By leveraging Rag programming techniques and adopting efficient workflow practices, you can streamline your deep learning development process, leading to faster model development and improved resource utilization.

7.3 Scaling Up Deep Learning: Integrating Langchain for Scalable Deep Learning Applications

Rag programming, with its ability to harness external knowledge, opens doors to powerful deep learning applications. However, dealing with massive datasets or complex models can pose computational challenges. This chapter explores Langchain, Rag programming's companion library, and its role in scaling up deep learning for demanding tasks.

The Bottlenecks of Scalability:

Data Deluge: Deep learning often thrives on vast amounts of data. Training models on such datasets can be time-consuming and resource-intensive on a single machine.

Model Complexity: As models become more intricate to handle complex tasks or incorporate knowledge infusion from Rag programming, training times can increase significantly.

Resource Constraints: Limited computational resources on a single machine might restrict the size and complexity of models you can train effectively.

_Langchain to the Rescue: Distributed Training with Rag Programming

Langchain empowers you to overcome these limitations by enabling distributed training and optimization for Rag programming and deep learning workflows. Here's how it breaks down:

Parallelization Power: Langchain can distribute training tasks across multiple machines or cores within a cluster. This parallelization approach significantly reduces training times, especially for computationally expensive models or large datasets.

Efficient Knowledge Access: Langchain's distributed architecture ensures efficient retrieval and processing of knowledge sources even in a distributed training setting. This is crucial, as Rag programming relies heavily on external knowledge for feature engineering.

Distributed Training with Langchain (placeholder code):

Python

```
#   (Placeholder   code)   Simulate   distributed
training with Langchain
```

```
def    train_model_distributed(model,    X_train,
y_train, num_workers):
    # Split data and knowledge source access among
worker processes
    # Leverage Langchain's distributed capabilities
to  train  the  model  in  parallel  across  multiple
workers
    # ... (implementation details)
    # Aggregate  training  results  from  all  workers
and update the model
    # ... (implementation details)
    return model


# Example  usage  (assuming  you  have  a  training
function for your deep learning model)
model = train_model(X_train, y_train)   # Regular
training
parallel_model   =   train_model_distributed(model,
X_train, y_train, num_workers=4)
```

Beyond Training: Distributed Hyperparameter Tuning

Langchain's capabilities extend beyond training. You can leverage
its distributed architecture to perform hyperparameter tuning more
efficiently:

Distributed Hyperparameter Search: Evaluate different
hyperparameter   configurations   on   multiple   machines
simultaneously, significantly reducing the time it takes to find the
optimal settings for your Rag programming model and deep
learning components.

Scalable Resource Allocation: With distributed training, you can
allocate resources more effectively. By dynamically assigning

workloads based on machine availability, Langchain helps ensure that your computational resources are utilized efficiently throughout the training and optimization process.

Benefits of Scalable Deep Learning with Langchain:

Reduced Training Times: By distributing the workload across multiple machines, Langchain can significantly accelerate the training process for deep learning models with Rag programming, allowing you to experiment more rapidly and iterate faster.

Handling Larger Datasets: Distributed training allows you to tackle datasets that would be impractical to handle on a single machine. This opens doors to working with richer and more comprehensive data sources, potentially leading to improved model performance.

Efficient Resource Utilization: Langchain optimizes resource allocation during training and hyperparameter tuning, ensuring you get the most out of your computational resources.

Advanced Techniques for Scalability:

As the field of distributed deep learning evolves, here are some exciting possibilities to explore:

Cloud-Based Training: Leverage cloud platforms that offer scalable compute resources to further accelerate training times for large-scale Rag programming and deep learning applications.

Integration with Distributed Deep Learning Frameworks: Explore frameworks like Horovod or TensorFlow Distributed for seamless integration with Langchain, enabling efficient distributed training across various hardware configurations.

By adopting distributed training and optimization techniques with Langchain, you can empower your Rag programming and deep learning projects to handle ever-growing datasets and complex models. This unlocks the full potential of knowledge-infused deep learning for real-world applications that demand scalability and performance.

Chapter 8:
Rag Programming Feasts for the Real World

In previous chapters, we explored the exciting potential of Rag programming and its companion library, Langchain. We delved into knowledge integration, deep learning applications, and efficient workflows. Now, it's time to explore the real-world applications of Rag programming and how it can be used to tackle various challenges across different domains.

A Buffet of Applications:

Rag programming's ability to leverage external knowledge opens doors to a diverse range of applications. Here are some examples to whet your appetite:

- **Enhanced Text Classification:** Imagine a system that classifies news articles not just by topic but also by sentiment or bias. Rag programming can incorporate knowledge about entities, events, and relationships to create more nuanced classifications.
- **Question Answering with Context:** Move beyond simple keyword matching in question answering systems. Rag programming can access knowledge graphs and factual databases to answer questions with rich context and reasoning.
- **Drug Discovery and Material Science:** Accelerate scientific discovery by incorporating knowledge from research papers, chemical databases, and material properties into machine learning models for drug discovery or material science applications.

- **Personalized Recommendations:** Recommender systems can benefit from Rag programming's ability to understand user preferences and context. By integrating knowledge about user demographics, past interactions, and relevant external information, Rag programming can create more personalized and relevant recommendations.
- **Financial Analysis and Fraud Detection:** Financial institutions can leverage Rag programming to analyze market trends, identify potential risks, and detect fraudulent activities. By incorporating knowledge about regulations, financial instruments, and historical data, Rag programming can enhance financial decision-making.

The Ingredients for Success:

While Rag programming offers a powerful toolkit, successful real-world applications require careful consideration of several factors:

- **Data Quality and Relevance:** The quality and relevance of both your primary data and the external knowledge sources are crucial for achieving optimal performance.
- **Knowledge Source Selection:** Choose knowledge sources that align well with your specific application domain and provide the most relevant information for your task.
- **Feature Engineering Expertise:** Extracting informative features from both data and knowledge sources requires careful design and domain knowledge.
- **Computational Resources:** Depending on the complexity of your model and the size of your data and knowledge sources, you might need access to substantial computational resources.

A Recipe for Success: Building Real-World Applications

Here's a general roadmap to guide you in developing real-world applications with Rag programming:

1. **Define your problem:** Clearly identify the task you want to address and the desired outcome of your application.
2. **Data Acquisition:** Gather relevant data for your task and identify appropriate knowledge sources that complement your data.
3. **Feature Engineering:** Design features that leverage both your data and knowledge sources. Utilize Rag programming functionalities for knowledge integration and feature extraction.
4. **Model Selection and Training:** Choose a suitable machine learning or deep learning model and train it using your engineered features. Consider techniques like distributed training with Langchain for large datasets or complex models.
5. **Evaluation and Refinement:** Evaluate your model's performance on unseen data and refine your approach based on the results. This might involve adjusting features, exploring different knowledge sources, or fine-tuning your model hyperparameters.

The Future Feast: Emerging Applications of Rag Programming

The field of Rag programming is constantly evolving. Here are some exciting possibilities on the horizon:

- **Lifelong Learning with Continuously Updated Knowledge:** Develop models that can continuously learn and improve by incorporating new knowledge from external sources as they become available.

- **Explainable AI with Knowledge Infusion:** Make AI models more interpretable by leveraging knowledge graphs and reasoning processes used during inference.
- **Integration with Emerging Technologies:** Explore the potential of combining Rag programming with cutting-edge technologies like natural language generation or reinforcement learning for even more powerful applications.

By embracing Rag programming and its unique capabilities, you can unlock a world of possibilities for building intelligent and knowledge-driven applications that address real-world challenges in various domains. Remember, the key is to leverage the power of both data and knowledge to create intelligent systems that can learn, reason, and make informed decisions.

8.1 From Cookbook to Restaurant: Utilizing Rag Programming in Finance, Healthcare, and More

Chapter 8 introduced the exciting potential of Rag programming for real-world applications across various domains. Now, let's delve deeper into specific use cases, exploring how Rag programming can be applied in the realms of finance, healthcare, and beyond.

Financial Feast: Rag Programming for Financial Applications

Enhanced Fraud Detection: Financial institutions grapple with various fraudulent activities. Rag programming can be a powerful tool in this fight.

_Scenario: Develop a system to detect fraudulent credit card transactions.

_Rag Programming in Action:

Access knowledge graphs containing information on fraudulent patterns, suspicious locations, and high-risk behaviors.

Extract features from transaction data (e.g., location, amount, time) and combine them with knowledge-based features (e.g., is the location associated with known fraudulent activity?).

Train a machine learning model to identify patterns indicative of fraud.

Stock Market Analysis with Knowledge Integration: Financial analysts strive to predict market trends. Rag programming can offer valuable insights.

Scenario: Build a model to predict stock prices based on news articles and company reports.

Rag Programming in Action:

Utilize Rag programming to process news articles and extract entities (companies, financial instruments) and relationships (mergers, acquisitions).

Leverage knowledge graphs containing financial data (historical prices, analyst ratings) and company information.

Combine features extracted from text data and knowledge sources to train a model for stock price prediction.

_Healthcare Helper: Rag Programming in Medical Applications

Drug Discovery with Knowledge Graphs: The drug discovery process is time-consuming and expensive. Rag programming can accelerate it.

Scenario: Develop a system to identify potential drug candidates for a specific disease.

Rag Programming in Action:

Access knowledge graphs containing information on diseases, genes, proteins, and existing drugs.

Analyze patient data (e.g., genetic information, symptoms) and link it to relevant entities in the knowledge graph.

Build a model to identify potential drug targets based on biological pathways and relationships within the knowledge graph.

Medical Diagnosis with Context: Accurate medical diagnosis is crucial. Rag programming can provide additional context.

Scenario: Develop a system to assist doctors in diagnosing complex medical conditions.

Rag Programming in Action:

Access knowledge graphs containing medical information about diseases, symptoms, and treatment options.

Analyze a patient's medical history and combine it with knowledge-based information about similar cases and potential diagnoses.

Present doctors with a ranked list of possible diagnoses along with relevant information from the knowledge graph to support decision-making.

Beyond Finance and Healthcare: Exploring Other Applications

The potential applications of Rag programming extend far beyond finance and healthcare. Here are some additional examples:

E-commerce and Retail: Build recommender systems that consider user preferences and product information to suggest relevant items.

Manufacturing and Quality Control: Analyze sensor data from machines and integrate knowledge about historical faults to predict and prevent equipment failures.

Media and Entertainment: Personalize content recommendations based on user profiles, movie genres, and actor relationships.

Social Media Analysis: Understand user sentiment and identify potential brand reputation issues by combining social media text data with knowledge about social trends and events.

Remember: These are just a few examples to inspire you. The possibilities for Rag programming applications are vast and depend on your creativity and the specific challenges you want to address.

_Key Considerations for Real-World Projects:

Data Availability and Quality: Ensure access to high-quality data relevant to your task and maintain a focus on data privacy and security when applicable.

Knowledge Source Selection: Choose knowledge sources that align with your domain and provide credible and up-to-date information.

Model Interpretability: Strive to build interpretable models, especially in domains like finance and healthcare, where understanding the reasoning behind decisions is crucial.

Human-in-the-Loop Approach: While Rag programming can automate tasks, human expertise remains essential. Design systems that leverage both machine intelligence and human oversight for optimal decision-making.

By following these guidelines and leveraging the unique capabilities of Rag programming, you can create intelligent systems that tackle complex problems and make a positive impact in various industries..

8.2 Serving Up Success: Best Practices for Deploying Rag Programming Solutions

Considerations for Deployment:

Model Serving Environment (placeholder code):

Python

```
# Example (cloud deployment using AWS SageMaker)
```

```python
from sagemaker.pytorch import PyTorchModel

# Assuming you have trained your Rag programming
model using PyTorch
model                                          =
PyTorchModel(model_data="s3://your-bucket/model.p
t", role="your-sagemaker-role")

# Deploy the model as an endpoint
endpoint = model.deploy(initial_instance_count=1,
instance_type="ml.m5.large")

# Make predictions using the deployed endpoint
(refer to SageMaker documentation for specific
calls)
predictions = endpoint.predict(...)
```

Remember: This is a simplified example using a specific cloud platform. The actual deployment code will vary depending on your chosen environment and framework.

Scalability and Performance: Monitor your deployed model's performance metrics (e.g., latency, throughput) and adjust resources accordingly. Cloud platforms often offer auto-scaling options.

Data Access and Security: Implement secure access controls and encryption mechanisms to protect data and knowledge sources in the deployment environment.

Monitoring and Maintainability: Utilize logging frameworks and monitoring tools to track model performance, data drift, and potential issues.

Serving Strategies for Rag Programming:

API Deployment (placeholder code):

Python

```python
from flask import Flask, request, jsonify

app = Flask(__name__)

@app.route("/predict", methods=["POST"])
def predict():
    # Load your Rag programming model
    model = ...    # Replace with your model loading
logic
    data = request.get_json()
    # Preprocess data and integrate knowledge using
Rag programming
                        processed_data          =
preprocess_and_integrate_knowledge(data)
    prediction = model.predict(processed_data)
    return jsonify({"prediction": prediction})

if __name__ == "__main__":
    app.run(host="0.0.0.0", port=5000)
```

Cloud-Based Deployment: Refer to the documentation of your chosen cloud platform (e.g., AWS SageMaker, Azure Machine Learning) for specific steps on deploying containerized models or serverless functions.

Containerization with Docker: Consider using tools like Docker to package your model, dependencies, and Rag programming components into a container for consistent execution across environments.

Best Practices for Successful Deployment:

Version Control: Use Git or a similar version control system to track changes in code, models, and knowledge sources.

Documentation: Create clear documentation for your deployed model, including:

Usage instructions

Expected inputs and outputs

Performance metrics

Maintenance procedures

Testing and Validation: Thoroughly test your deployed model in a staging environment before making it publicly available.

Continuous Improvement: Monitor your model's performance in production and gather user feedback. Use this information to refine your model over time.

Additional Considerations:

Explainability in Production: Explore techniques like LIME or SHAP to explain model predictions even in production.

Ethical Considerations: Implement fairness checks and mitigation strategies to address potential biases in your data or knowledge sources.

By following these best practices and carefully considering the deployment environment, you can ensure your Rag programming solutions are effectively served, delivering value to users and addressing real-world challenges responsibly.

8.3 Troubleshooting Your Dish: Common Challenges and Techniques for Rag Programming

Challenge #1: Data Quality and Relevance

Issue: Poor data quality or data misalignment with the knowledge source can lead to inaccurate results.

Technique:

Data Cleaning (placeholder code):

Python

```python
import pandas as pd

# Load your data
data = pd.read_csv("your_data.csv")

# Handle missing values
```

```python
data = data.fillna(data.mean())    # Replace with
appropriate imputation strategy

# Identify and address inconsistencies (replace
with specific checks based on your data)
data = data[data["column1"] > 0]    # Example
filter for invalid values

# ... (Perform additional cleaning steps as
needed)
```

Data Relevance Evaluation: Analyze your data and chosen knowledge source to ensure they address the same entities, concepts, and relationships relevant to your task.

Data Augmentation (placeholder code):

Python

```python
from nltk.corpus import wordnet

# Example: Synonym replacement for text
augmentation
def synonym_augmentation(text):
  words = text.split()
                          synonyms          =
[wordnet.synsets(w)[0].synonyms()[0].name() for w
in words]
  return " ".join(synonyms)
```

```
augmented_data = [synonym_augmentation(text) for
text in data["text_column"]]
```

Challenge #2: Knowledge Source Selection and Integration

Issue: Inappropriate knowledge source or challenges in integrating knowledge can affect model performance.

Technique:

Knowledge Source Selection: Research and select knowledge sources that are:

Domain-specific

Credible

Well-maintained

Aligned with your data schema (e.g., entity types, relationships)

Knowledge Integration Techniques: Explore different approaches like:

Entity linking: Linking entities in your data to corresponding entities in the knowledge source.

Relation extraction: Extracting relationships between entities from the knowledge source.

Schema Consistency: Ensure consistency between the data schema (e.g., column names, data types) and the structure of information within the knowledge source (e.g., entity properties, relation types).

Challenge #3: Feature Engineering and Model Selection

Issue: Uninformative features or unsuitable models can lead to subpar performance.

Technique:

Feature Engineering Exploration: Try different techniques like:

Word embeddings (e.g., Word2Vec, GloVe) to capture semantic relationships between words.

Topic modeling (e.g., Latent Dirichlet Allocation) to identify latent topics in text data.

Feature Importance Analysis: Utilize libraries like scikit-learn to calculate feature importances and identify the most influential features for your model.

Model Selection and Comparison: Experiment with different machine learning models (e.g., logistic regression, random forest) or deep learning architectures (e.g., convolutional neural networks, recurrent neural networks) to find the best fit for your data and task.

Challenge #4: Model Training and Overfitting

Issue: Training issues like overfitting or slow convergence can prevent the model from learning effectively.

Technique:

Regularization (placeholder code):

Python

```python
from sklearn.linear_model import LogisticRegression

# Train a logistic regression model with L2 regularization
model = LogisticRegression(penalty="l2", C=0.1)
# Adjust hyperparameter (C) as needed
model.fit(X_train, y_train)
```

Early Stopping (placeholder code):

Python

```python
from tensorflow.keras.callbacks import EarlyStopping

# Early stopping callback to halt training if validation performance plateaus
early_stopping = EarlyStopping(monitor="val_loss", patience=3)
```

```
model.fit(X_train,                                    y_train,
validation_data=(X_val,       y_val),       epochs=10,
callbacks=[early_stopping])
```

Data Augmentation and Curriculum Learning: Explore these
techniques to improve training efficiency and prevent overfitting.

Challenge #5: Model Explainability and Debugging

Issue: Difficulty in understanding how the model leverages
knowledge or interpreting its decision-making process can hinder
debugging and improvement.

Chapter 9:

A Glimpse into the Future: The Evolving World of Rag Programming

Rag programming, with its ability to harness external knowledge, has opened doors to powerful deep learning applications. As the field continues to evolve, exciting possibilities are emerging that will shape the future of this technology. Let's delve into some of these advancements:

1. Lifelong Learning with Continuously Updated Knowledge:

Current Rag programming models typically rely on static knowledge sources. Imagine models that can continuously learn and improve by incorporating new knowledge from external sources as it becomes available.

- **Real-World Applications:**
    - Financial forecasting models that adapt to changing market conditions and economic data.
    - Medical diagnosis systems that integrate the latest medical research findings.
    - Scientific discovery tools that leverage newly published research papers and datasets.
- **Technical Advancements:**
    - Incremental learning algorithms that allow models to efficiently update their knowledge base with new information.
    - Knowledge graph embedding techniques that facilitate the integration of new knowledge entities and relationships into existing knowledge graphs.

2. Explainable AI with Knowledge Infusion:

Many AI models, including those built with Rag programming, can be opaque in their decision-making processes. This lack of explainability can hinder trust and adoption. The future lies in explainable AI (XAI) techniques that leverage Rag programming's knowledge integration capabilities.

- **Real-World Applications:**
  - Recommender systems that explain why specific items are recommended to users.
  - Medical diagnosis systems that provide reasoning behind diagnoses based on the knowledge graph.
  - Financial fraud detection systems that explain the rationale for flagging suspicious transactions.
- **Technical Advancements:**
  - Integrating attention mechanisms into Rag programming models to identify the specific knowledge elements used in making predictions.
  - Developing counterfactual explanation techniques that explore alternative scenarios based on the knowledge graph to explain model decisions.

3. Integration with Emerging Technologies:

The future of Rag programming is not confined to deep learning. By combining it with cutting-edge technologies, we can unlock even more powerful applications.

- **Natural Language Generation (NLG):** Imagine Rag programming models that not only analyze information but also generate human-readable text reports or explanations based on their knowledge and reasoning processes.
- **Reinforcement Learning (RL):** Combine Rag programming's knowledge access with RL agents to create intelligent systems that can learn through trial and error while leveraging external knowledge for better decision-making.

4. Democratization of Rag Programming:

Currently, Rag programming requires some technical expertise. The future holds promise for more user-friendly tools and libraries that allow a broader range of users to leverage its power.

- **Visual Programming Interfaces:** Develop graphical interfaces that allow users to define knowledge sources, feature engineering pipelines, and model configurations without writing code.
- **AutoML Integration:** Integrate Rag programming functionalities with AutoML tools to automate hyperparameter tuning and model selection for knowledge-infused deep learning workflows.

The Road Ahead:

The future of Rag programming is bright. As the field continues to evolve, we can expect advancements in areas like lifelong learning, explainability, and integration with emerging technologies. By making Rag programming more accessible and user-friendly, we can empower a wider range of users to leverage its potential and unlock its power for solving real-world problems across various domains.

Remember: This glimpse into the future is just the beginning. As research and development progress, the possibilities for Rag programming are limitless. By embracing innovation and collaboration, we can shape the future of AI towards a more knowledge-driven and intelligent world.

Chapter 9 provided a glimpse into the exciting future of Rag programming. Here, we delve deeper into specific trends and advancements that are shaping the landscape of this powerful technology.

1. Lifelong Learning with Continuously Updated Knowledge

Imagine AI models that constantly learn and improve, not just from data but also by incorporating the latest knowledge from external sources. This future of Rag programming holds immense potential for various applications:

Evolving Financial Models: Financial forecasting models that adapt to dynamic market conditions and integrate new economic data can provide more accurate predictions.

Self-Improving Medical Diagnosis Systems: Medical diagnosis systems that continuously learn from the latest medical research findings can offer more comprehensive and up-to-date diagnoses.

Scientific Discovery at Scale: Scientific discovery tools that leverage newly published research papers and datasets can accelerate scientific progress by identifying promising areas for further investigation.

Technical Advancements for Lifelong Learning:

Incremental Learning Algorithms: Researchers are developing algorithms that allow models to efficiently update their knowledge base with new information without retraining on the entire dataset from scratch.

Knowledge Graph Embedding Techniques: Advancements in knowledge graph embedding techniques will facilitate the seamless integration of new knowledge entities and relationships into existing knowledge graphs, enabling models to reason over a broader and more comprehensive knowledge base.

2. Explainable AI with Knowledge Infusion

The lack of explainability in many AI models, including Rag programming models, can be a barrier to trust and adoption. The future lies in explainable AI (XAI) techniques that leverage Rag programming's ability to integrate knowledge:

Reasoning-based Explanations: Imagine Rag programming models that explain their predictions by highlighting the specific knowledge elements (entities, relationships) from the knowledge graph used in the reasoning process.

Counterfactual Explanations: Advancements in XAI can allow Rag programming models to provide counterfactual explanations. These explanations explore alternative scenarios based on the knowledge graph to demonstrate how different knowledge or data could have led to different predictions, fostering greater understanding of the model's decision-making process.

Real-World Applications:

Users can gain deeper insights into why recommender systems suggest specific items.

Medical professionals can receive explanations behind diagnoses based on the knowledge graph, leading to more informed treatment decisions.

Financial institutions can understand the rationale for flagging suspicious transactions in fraud detection systems.

3. Integration with Cutting-Edge Technologies

Rag programming's potential extends beyond deep learning. By combining it with emerging technologies, we can create even more powerful AI systems:

Natural Language Generation (NLG): Imagine a future where Rag programming models not only analyze information but also generate human-readable reports or justifications for their decisions based on the knowledge they leverage. This can be crucial for building trust and understanding in applications like loan approvals or risk assessments.

Reinforcement Learning (RL): Merging Rag programming's knowledge access with RL agents can create intelligent systems that learn through trial and error while using external knowledge for informed decision-making. This could lead to breakthroughs in areas like robotics and autonomous systems navigation.

4. Democratization of Rag Programming

Currently, Rag programming requires some technical expertise. The future holds promise for advancements that make this technology more accessible to a wider range of users:

Visual Programming Interfaces: Development of graphical user interfaces (GUIs) would allow users to define knowledge sources, feature engineering pipelines, and model configurations without writing code. This can empower domain experts to leverage Rag programming's power without needing extensive programming knowledge.

AutoML Integration: Integrating Rag programming functionalities with AutoML tools can automate hyperparameter tuning and model selection for knowledge-infused deep learning workflows. This would streamline the development process and make Rag programming more accessible to users with less machine learning expertise.

The Future is Bright

As research and development progress, Rag programming's capabilities will continue to evolve. By embracing these emerging trends and advancements, we can unlock the full potential of Rag programming to address complex challenges in various fields and contribute to a future where AI is not only powerful but also understandable and trustworthy.

9.2 The Role of Langchain: Exploring Langchain's Role in Next-Generation Data Science

Langchain, Rag programming's companion library, plays a vital role in unlocking the potential of this revolutionary approach to AI.

As we explored the future of Rag programming in the previous chapter, let's delve deeper into how Langchain contributes to the advancements in next-generation data science.

1. Distributed Training and Scalability

Langchain's distributed training capabilities are essential for handling the ever-growing volume and complexity of data used in modern AI applications. Here's how it contributes to next-generation data science:

Large-Scale Knowledge Integration: Training Rag programming models often involves integrating vast knowledge sources. Langchain enables distributed processing of these knowledge sources, making it feasible to handle massive knowledge graphs and datasets.

Efficient Model Training: By distributing training tasks across multiple machines or cores, Langchain accelerates the training process for complex Rag programming models. This allows data scientists to experiment more rapidly and iterate faster on different model architectures and knowledge integration techniques.

Resource Optimization: Langchain ensures efficient resource allocation during training. It can dynamically assign workloads based on machine availability, maximizing the utilization of computational resources within a cluster or cloud environment.

2. Collaborative Knowledge Workflows

Langchain facilitates collaboration among data scientists and domain experts working on Rag programming projects. Here's how it contributes to next-generation data science:

Modular Knowledge Source Management: Langchain allows researchers to define and manage knowledge sources in a modular way. This enables collaboration where domain experts can contribute their knowledge expertise by creating and maintaining specific knowledge modules without needing deep programming knowledge.

Version Control and Reproducibility: Langchain integrates with version control systems, allowing teams to track changes in knowledge sources, models, and code. This ensures reproducibility and facilitates collaboration by enabling researchers to revert to previous versions if needed.

Standardized Knowledge Representation: Langchain promotes the use of standardized knowledge representation formats. This allows researchers to share and reuse knowledge sources across different projects, fostering collaboration and accelerating scientific progress.

3. Lifelong Learning and Knowledge Graph Evolution

Next-generation data science demands models that continuously learn and adapt. Langchain plays a key role in supporting this vision:

Incremental Knowledge Updates: Langchain's architecture facilitates the integration of new knowledge into existing knowledge graphs. This enables Rag programming models to leverage the latest information and adapt to evolving data landscapes.

Knowledge Graph Refinement: Langchain allows researchers to define mechanisms for refining and updating knowledge graphs over time. This can involve techniques like identifying and correcting inconsistencies or incorporating user feedback to improve the quality and accuracy of the knowledge base.

4. Foundation for Explainable AI

Explainability is crucial for trust and adoption of AI models. Langchain lays the groundwork for building explainable Rag programming systems:

Knowledge Provenance Tracking: Langchain can track the lineage of knowledge used in making predictions. This allows researchers to understand how specific entities, relationships, and reasoning steps within the knowledge graph contributed to a particular model output.

Counterfactual Explanations with Langchain: Langchain's ability to manage different versions of knowledge graphs can be leveraged to generate counterfactual explanations. By simulating how different knowledge configurations might have influenced the model's output, Langchain can provide deeper insights into the model's decision-making process.

Langchain: A Powerful Ally

Langchain is not just a distributed training library; it's a foundational element for building robust and scalable knowledge-infused AI systems. By addressing challenges in knowledge management, collaboration, and explainability, Langchain empowers data scientists to unlock the full potential of Rag programming and contribute to the future of intelligent systems.

As research in Rag programming and Langchain continues, we can expect even more exciting advancements that will reshape the landscape of data science and artificial intelligence.

9.3 Staying on the Menu: Resources for Keeping Up-to-Date with Rag Programming

The field of Rag programming is rapidly evolving, and staying current with the latest advancements can be crucial for researchers and practitioners alike. Here are some valuable resources to help you stay on top of the game:

Online Communities and Forums:

Hugging Face Rag Programming Community Forum: https://huggingface.co/docs/transformers/en/model_doc/rag - Engage with a community of Rag programming enthusiasts, researchers, and developers. Discuss projects, share ideas, and ask questions.

The AI Stack Exchange: https://ai.stackexchange.com/ - Pose technical questions related to Rag programming and deep learning on this popular forum. Benefit from the expertise of a broad AI community.

Reddit Machine Learning: https://www.reddit.com/r/MachineLearning/ - Join discussions on Rag programming and related topics on the machine learning subreddit. Explore trends, news, and user experiences.

Research Papers and Articles:

Browse research papers on Rag programming: Utilize academic search engines like Google Scholar or arXiv to find the latest research papers on Rag programming. Explore specific areas of interest within the field, such as lifelong learning or explainability in Rag programming models. (Use a general search engine to find these resources).

Follow relevant publications: Subscribe to journals and conferences that publish research on knowledge-infused deep learning and Rag programming. Stay informed about cutting-edge advancements presented at major AI conferences.

Tutorials and Courses:

Rag programming tutorials on Hugging Face: https://huggingface.co/docs/transformers/en/model_doc/rag - Leverage tutorials and resources provided by Hugging Face, a prominent player in the field of transformers and deep learning. Learn about core Rag programming concepts and practical implementation techniques.

Online courses on knowledge-infused deep learning: Explore online course platforms like Coursera, Udacity, or edX for courses on knowledge graphs, reasoning with external knowledge, and related topics that can strengthen your foundation in Rag programming.

Open-Source Projects:

Explore Rag programming implementations on GitHub: GitHub is a treasure trove of open-source projects. Search for Rag programming repositories to explore code implementations, experiment with different approaches, and learn from the work of others. (Use a general search engine to find this resource).

Langchain library repository: https://github.com/langchain-ai/langchain - delve into the Langchain library's codebase to understand how it facilitates distributed training, knowledge source management, and other functionalities essential for Rag programming projects.

Keeping the Momentum Going:

The resources listed above provide a solid starting point for your Rag programming journey. Remember, staying up-to-date requires ongoing exploration and engagement. Here are some additional tips:

Attend webinars and conferences: Participate in online or in-person events related to Rag programming and deep learning. Network with other researchers and practitioners, learn from expert talks, and stay updated on the latest trends.

Follow thought leaders: Identify prominent researchers and figures actively contributing to the field of Rag programming. Follow their blogs, articles, or social media feeds to gain insights from their work.

Contribute to the community: As you gain expertise, consider sharing your knowledge by writing blog posts, creating tutorials, or participating in discussions on forums. Contributing to the community fosters collaboration and accelerates advancements.

By actively engaging with these resources and staying curious, you can ensure that your knowledge of Rag programming stays fresh and relevant. As the field continues to evolve, you'll be well-positioned to leverage its potential and contribute to the future of intelligent systems.

This concludes our exploration of Rag programming, a revolutionary approach to AI that harnesses external knowledge to empower deep learning models. Throughout this journey, you've gained a comprehensive understanding of its core concepts, implementation techniques, and the exciting future that lies ahead.

The Power of Combining Knowledge and Learning

Rag programming bridges the gap between traditional deep learning and symbolic AI. By enabling models to leverage structured knowledge from external sources, it unlocks new possibilities for AI applications. Here's why Rag programming expertise is valuable:

- **Enhanced Reasoning Capabilities:** Models equipped with knowledge can reason and make informed decisions beyond simple pattern recognition in data. This opens doors to complex tasks requiring a deeper understanding of the world.
- **Improved Generalizability:** Knowledge-infused models can generalize better to unseen data by leveraging their understanding of concepts and relationships within the knowledge graph. This leads to more robust and reliable AI systems.
- **Explainability and Trust:** Rag programming allows for a deeper understanding of how models arrive at their predictions. By tracing the reasoning steps based on the knowledge graph, we can build more explainable and trustworthy AI.

Unlocking Potential Across Domains

The power of Rag programming extends beyond theoretical concepts. Its applications can have a significant impact on various domains:

- **Scientific Discovery:** Imagine AI systems that can analyze scientific literature and knowledge graphs to accelerate research by identifying promising areas for investigation.
- **Healthcare:** Knowledge-infused models can assist doctors in diagnosis, treatment planning, and drug discovery by leveraging vast medical knowledge bases.
- **Finance:** Rag programming holds promise for building intelligent financial models that consider market trends, economic data, and financial regulations for more accurate forecasting and investment decisions.
- **Natural Language Processing (NLP):** By integrating knowledge about grammar, semantics, and real-world entities, Rag programming can enhance the capabilities of NLP tasks like question answering and sentiment analysis.

A Call to Action: Sharpening Your Rag Programming Skills

As the field of Rag programming continues to evolve, the demand for skilled practitioners will rise. Here's how you can hone your expertise:

- **Deepen your foundational knowledge:** Ensure a strong understanding of deep learning concepts, machine learning algorithms, and knowledge representation techniques.
- **Practice with open-source libraries:** Explore libraries like Hugging Face Transformers and Langchain to gain practical experience with Rag programming model development and deployment.

- **Contribute to open-source projects:** Participating in open-source projects is a great way to learn from others, contribute to the community, and build a strong portfolio.
- **Stay updated with advancements:** Continuously learn about the latest research and developments in the field. Utilize the resources discussed in Chapter 9.3 to stay on top of the game.

The Future is Bright for Rag Programming Experts

The future of AI holds immense potential for Rag programming. As you continue to develop your expertise, you'll be well-positioned to play a critical role in shaping this future. By leveraging your knowledge to build intelligent systems that combine the power of deep learning with the richness of external knowledge, you can contribute to solving real-world challenges and pushing the boundaries of what AI can achieve.

Remember: The journey of learning is continuous. Embrace the constant evolution of Rag programming, and use your expertise to build a brighter future powered by intelligent and knowledge-driven AI.

10.1 A Recap of Your Culinary Journey: Key Learnings and Gained Expertise

Throughout this delightful exploration, you've embarked on a journey as a Rag programming chef, mastering the art of crafting intelligent systems that leverage external knowledge. Now, as you reach the dessert course, let's savor the key learnings and expertise you've gained:

The Essential Ingredients:

Deep Learning Foundations: You've established a strong understanding of deep learning concepts like neural networks, transformers, and various machine learning algorithms – the building blocks of your Rag programming creations.

Knowledge Representation: You've explored different knowledge representation techniques like knowledge graphs, allowing you to structure external information in a way that AI models can understand and reason over.

Rag Programming Techniques: You've grasped the core functionalities of Rag programming, including knowledge integration methods, model architectures, and training strategies. You can now effectively combine deep learning with external knowledge sources.

The Art of Integration:

Feature Engineering: You've learned how to transform data and knowledge graph elements into informative features, the key ingredients for training your Rag programming models.

Model Selection and Training: You can now choose appropriate deep learning architectures and tailor training processes to create Rag programming models that excel at specific tasks.

The Finishing Touches:

Deployment and Serving: You've explored strategies for deploying your Rag programming models in real-world environments, ensuring they can effectively serve users and deliver value.

Troubleshooting and Debugging: You've equipped yourself with techniques to identify and address challenges that may arise during Rag programming development.

A World of Flavors: Applications and Potential

Enhanced Reasoning: You understand how Rag programming empowers models to reason and make informed decisions beyond simple data patterns, unlocking possibilities for complex tasks.

Improved Generalizability: Knowledge-infused models can now leverage their understanding from the knowledge graph to generalize better to unseen data, leading to more robust and reliable AI systems.

Explainability and Trust: You've explored how Rag programming fosters explainable AI by allowing us to trace the reasoning steps based on the knowledge graph, building trust in AI models.

The Future of the Menu: Sharpening Your Skills

With your newfound expertise, you're ready to take your Rag programming skills to the next level:

Deepen Foundational Knowledge: Continuously strengthen your understanding of deep learning, machine learning, and knowledge representation to stay ahead of the curve.

Hands-on Practice: Dive into practical experience by working with open-source libraries like Hugging Face Transformers and

Langchain. Experiment with model development, deployment, and explore creative applications.

Open Source Contribution: Consider contributing to open-source projects. This fosters collaboration, allows you to learn from others, and showcases your expertise to the community.

Staying Updated: Actively engage with the Rag programming community through forums, research papers, and online courses. Embrace lifelong learning to stay current with the latest advancements.

The Final Course: A Seat at the AI Table

The future of AI is brimming with possibilities for Rag programming experts. As you continue to refine your skills, you'll be well-positioned to:

Build Intelligent Systems: Develop AI systems that combine the power of deep learning with the vastness of external knowledge, tackling real-world challenges across various domains.

Shape the Future of AI: By leveraging your Rag programming expertise, you can contribute to shaping the future of AI, fostering the development of intelligent and knowledge-driven systems.

Remember: The world of Rag programming is constantly evolving. Embrace the journey of continuous learning and use your expertise to create a future powered by intelligent and insightful AI.

Having mastered the foundational concepts of Rag programming, you're now eager to experiment and push the boundaries of your knowledge. This section serves as your culinary reference guide, packed with valuable resources to fuel your exploration and propel your Rag programming expertise to new heights.

1. Delving Deeper into the Code:

Hugging Face Transformers Library: https://huggingface.co/transformers - This comprehensive library provides pre-trained transformer models and tools specifically designed for building and deploying Rag programming models. Explore their documentation, tutorials, and community forums to delve deeper into the code and gain practical experience.

Langchain Codebase: https://github.com/langchain-ai/langchain - Langchain, Rag programming's companion library, is instrumental for distributed training and knowledge source management. By studying its codebase on Github, you can gain a deeper understanding of its functionalities and how it facilitates efficient Rag programming workflows.

Open-Source Rag Programming Projects: Explore platforms like GitHub (https://github.com/) to discover a treasure trove of open-source Rag programming projects. Scrutinize the code implementations used in these projects. This not only allows you to learn from different approaches but also provides a foundation for building your own Rag programming applications.

2. Expanding Your Knowledge Buffet:

Research Papers and Articles: Stay at the forefront of advancements by actively searching for research papers on Rag programming. Utilize academic search engines like Google Scholar or arXiv to explore specific areas of interest, such as lifelong learning or explainable AI in Rag programming models.

Follow Influential Publications: Subscribe to prominent journals and conferences that publish cutting-edge research on knowledge-infused deep learning and Rag programming. Stay informed about the latest breakthroughs presented at major AI conferences.

3. Refining Your Skills Through Practice:

Rag Programming Tutorials: Sharpen your practical skills by working through tutorials offered by Hugging Face (https://huggingface.co/docs/transformers/en/index) and other online learning platforms. These tutorials provide hands-on guidance on core Rag programming concepts and implementation techniques.

Online Courses on Knowledge-Infused Deep Learning: Consider enrolling in online courses offered by platforms like Coursera, Udacity, or edX. These courses can provide a structured learning environment to strengthen your foundation in knowledge graphs, reasoning with external knowledge, and related topics that are crucial for Rag programming expertise.

4. Engaging with the Rag Programming Community:

Hugging Face Rag Programming Community Forum: https://huggingface.co/docs/transformers/en/model_doc/rag -

Actively participate in discussions on the Hugging Face Rag programming forum. Connect with other enthusiasts, researchers, and developers. Share your projects, ask questions, and gain valuable insights from the community.

The AI Stack Exchange: https://ai.stackexchange.com/ - Pose technical questions related to Rag programming and deep learning on this popular forum. Benefit from the collective knowledge and expertise of a broad AI community.

Reddit Machine Learning: https://www.reddit.com/r/MachineLearning/ - Join discussions on Rag programming and related topics on the machine learning subreddit. Explore trends, news, user experiences, and stay updated on the latest developments in the field.

5. Contributing to the Future of Rag Programming:

Open-Source Project Participation: Consider contributing to open-source Rag programming projects on GitHub. This allows you to give back to the community, collaborate with others, and showcase your expertise. Remember, open-source contribution is a two-way street; you'll also learn from experienced developers and gain valuable insights into real-world Rag programming applications.

Blogging and Knowledge Sharing: As you gain proficiency, consider creating blog posts, tutorials, or even video content to share your Rag programming knowledge with the community. This not only establishes you as a thought leader but also fosters collaboration and accelerates advancements in the field.

By actively engaging with these resources and cultivating a growth mindset, you'll ensure your Rag programming expertise stays fresh and relevant. Remember, the journey of learning is continuous. Embrace the ever-evolving nature of Rag programming, and use your knowledge to create a future powered by intelligent and insightful AI systems.

10.3 The Master Chef's Touch: Final Thoughts on the Power of Rag Programming Expertise

Congratulations! You've reached the final chapter of this culinary exploration of Rag programming. As you stand tall, a master chef in the realm of AI, it's time to reflect on the power of the knowledge you've gained and the exciting possibilities that lie ahead.

Rag Programming: A Paradigm Shift in AI

Rag programming represents a significant leap forward in the field of AI. By enabling models to leverage external knowledge, it opens doors to a new era of intelligent systems capable of reasoning, adapting, and understanding the world in a more nuanced way.

The Impact of Your Expertise

As a Rag programming expert, you possess a valuable skillset that can significantly impact various domains:

Scientific Discovery: Your expertise can aid in developing AI systems that can analyze vast amounts of scientific literature and knowledge graphs, accelerating research and innovation.

Healthcare: You can contribute to building intelligent healthcare systems that leverage medical knowledge bases to improve diagnosis, treatment planning, and drug discovery.

Finance: Your skills can be instrumental in creating robust financial models that consider market trends, economic data, and regulations, leading to more informed investment decisions.

Natural Language Processing (NLP): By integrating knowledge about grammar, semantics, and real-world entities, you can help develop advanced NLP applications for tasks like question answering and sentiment analysis.

A Shared Future: Shaping the Landscape of AI

The potential applications of Rag programming are vast and constantly evolving. As you continue to hone your expertise, you'll play a pivotal role in shaping the future of AI:

Building Explainable Systems: Your knowledge of Rag programming can contribute to the development of more explainable AI models, fostering trust and transparency in AI advancements.

Addressing Real-World Challenges: By applying your skills to specific problems, you can develop intelligent systems that tackle complex real-world challenges across various sectors.

Guiding Responsible AI Development: Your expertise can be crucial in ensuring the responsible development and deployment of Rag programming models, mitigating potential biases and safety concerns.

The Final Course: A Call to Continuous Learning

The world of Rag programming is brimming with potential, but it's also a field undergoing rapid evolution. Here are some parting words to guide you on your continuous learning journey:

Stay Curious: Maintain a thirst for knowledge. Actively seek out new research, advancements, and applications of Rag programming.

Embrace Collaboration: The AI community thrives on collaboration. Share your knowledge, contribute to open-source projects, and learn from others.

Never Stop Experimenting: Don't be afraid to experiment with new ideas and approaches. Push the boundaries of Rag programming and explore its potential in uncharted territories.

As you embark on this exciting journey of continuous learning, remember the power you hold as a Rag programming expert. With dedication, collaboration, and a dash of creativity, you can use your skills to build a future powered by intelligent and knowledge-driven AI, shaping a world where AI plays a positive and impactful role.

Bon appétit on your journey of mastering Rag programming!